MUNICIPAL CONTROL OF PUBLIC UTILITIES

A Study of the Attitude of our Courts toward an
Increase of the Sphere of Municipal Activity

BY

OSCAR LEWIS POND

AMS PRESS
NEW YORK

COLUMBIA UNIVERSITY
STUDIES IN THE
SOCIAL SCIENCES

65

The Series was formerly known as
Studies in History, Economics and Public Law.

Reprinted with the permission of Columbia University Press
From the edition of 1906, New York
First AMS EDITION published 1968
Manufactured in the United States of America

Library of Congress Catalogue Card Number: 79-76676

AMS PRESS, INC.
NEW YORK, N. Y. 10003

CONTENTS

CHAPTER I

INTRODUCTION

ONE of the most marked characteristics of American as of European civilization is the great development of urban life. This development has been not only extensive but intensive. Cities have increased not only in number but also in size, and not only are the problems incident to urban life becoming of interest to greater and still greater numbers of persons but the solution of these problems is at the same time becoming more difficult and more necessary.

One of the methods of solving these problems is the extension of the sphere of municipal activity. At one time our conception of a city, similar to our conception of the government as a whole, was that it was an organization which should preserve order and, within the limits of the law which it was its duty to enforce, permit the greatest possible freedom of action to the individual, from whose initiative and energetic activity it was believed that the community as a whole would derive the utmost advantage.

It was found, however, that unregulated or insufficiently regulated individual activity was followed in the life of our urban communities by such evils that it became necessary to have greater and greater recourse to the repressive activity of municipal as well as state governmental organs. Such repressive activity was believed at first in many instances to be inconsistent with the guarantees of individual rights contained in our constitutions. But our courts, to which appeal was had by those who thought that their constitutional rights were being violated through the increase in the activity of our governments, decided that all individuals held their rights subject to the regulatory power of the state. They elaborated what was called the police power through the exercise of which the community could, notwithstanding constitutional provision, protect itself against the undue emphasis by the individual on what he regarded as his constitutional rights.

Of late years, however, it has come to be believed by many that a due consideration for the rights of the community and the proper promotion of the public welfare are not secured through the mere repressive action of our governments and that on the contrary the only way in which the greatest advantage to the public as a whole can be secured is through the positive action of our governmental agencies by offering greater opportunities to the masses to better both their physical and their spiritual conditions.

Inasmuch as the problems of our modern civilization become more acute in the most complex conditions which exist and which are to be found in our cities, this demand for the extension of governmental activity has naturally assumed the form of a demand for the municipal ownership and operation of what have come to be known as municipal public utilities.

But just as when the demand was made for the extension of the repressive activity of government, it was alleged that such action was prohibited by our constitutional provisions protecting private rights, so now it is claimed that the system of municipal government outlined in our constitutions and in our law of municipal corporations is of a distinctly governmental character, as it is sometimes called, and does not permit the city as we know it to enter into the field of what is denominated as private business. The city in our system, it has been said, is organized for government and not for profit. Its activity should therefore be confined to those purposes which, because their pursuit is unprofitable, will not be undertaken by private effort; and profitable undertakings must be left to such private effort which will both undertake all that is necessary and do what is done better than the city can be expected to do it.

It is to answer the legal questions raised by such a claim that the following inquiry is undertaken. In order to accomplish the purpose, which has thus been outlined, the attempt has been made to ascertain both the nature of the city organization as expressed in the law and the construction placed by the courts on the powers given to cities; to discover what are the limitations on municipal activity which are contained in our constitutions, as construed by the courts, and how far the judicial construction of the law with regard to the taxation and sale of the property of cities aids or hampers the cities in the discharge of the new duties which they may be called upon to assume; and finally to ascertain what are the powers of control possessed by cities over the operation by private individuals of those public utilities which it is deemed wise to leave in private hands.

While it is not intended to anticipate here the results of this inquiry, it may not perhaps be amiss to say that the courts have again shown themselves to be regardful of the necessity of changing our conceptions of what is the proper sphere of governmental activity when the change in our economic and social conditions has seemed to make such a change necessary. As in the past they developed the idea of a repressive police power whose exercise was not inconsistent with constitutional private rights, so now they have elaborated the doctrine of implied powers through whose application the cities may be recognized as possessing powers which at one time would probably not have been regarded as theirs.

CHAPTER II

The Two Capacities of Municipal Corporations

Municipal corporations, like all others, are creatures of statutory origin and possess only the powers, granted to them by the legislature. These powers consist of those granted in express words; those necessarily or fairly implied in or incident to the powers expressly granted; and those essential to the declared objects and purposes of the corporation—not simply convenient, but indispensable.[1]

The powers with which municipal corporations are thus endowed are of two main classes and bring it about that municipal corporations act in two distinct capacities. The one is governmental, legislative or public; the other is proprietary and essentially business or commercial. As an agent of the state which creates it the municipality administers justice, attends to the preservation of the public peace, and performs other duties, essentially public and governmental.[2] On the other hand, in the enforcement of many of its own by-laws, in the erection and operation of gas works, electric-light plants, and waterworks and in attending to matters of local interest merely the corporation acts as a business concern.[3]

Over all the public or governmental powers exercised

[1] Dillon, *Municipal Corporations*, sec. 89 and cases cited.

[2] Springfield Fire & Marine Ins. Co. *vs.* Keeseville, 148 N. Y., 46; Illinois Trust & Savings Bank *vs.* Arkansas City, 76 Fed., 271.

[3] City of Henderson *vs.* Young, 83 S. W., 583; Port Jervis Water Co. *vs.* Port Jervis, 151 N. Y., 111; The City of Indianapolis *vs.* The Indianapolis Gas, etc., Co., 66 Ind., 396; Blood *vs.* Electric Co., 68 N. H., 340.

by the city in its capacity as an agent of the state
the authority of the state is from the nature of the
relation between it and the city, essentially supreme, in
the absence of constitutional limitations. The rule of
law is well established that municipal corporations have
no authority to make contracts for the discharge of a
purely public governmental duty. Such governmental
functions and powers must be left free and untram-
meled so that they may be exercised for the benefit of
the citizens as the emergencies may arise.[1]　A city for
example cannot make a contract with the owner of a building to put out a fire therein and then require him to pay
for such service, nor can it expose itself to liability if it
fails to put out the fire with regard to which it has attempted
to make the contract. The municipality cannot abridge its
legislative power by contract. The case of Brick Presbyterian Church *vs.* City of New York [2] states the reason for
this rule of law. The action in the case was for breach of
covenant for the quiet enjoyment of premises which the
defendant city had leased to the plaintiff for church and
cemetery purposes. After making the lease and pursuant
to a statute the city by ordinance prohibited the use of
such premises for a cemetery. In refusing relief on the
ground that the city had no power to limit its legislative
discretion by covenant the court said: " Sixty years ago,
when the lease was made, the premises were beyond the
inhabited parts of the city. They were a common; and
bounded on one side by a vineyard. Now they are in the
very heart of the city. When the defendant covenanted
that the lessees might enjoy the premises for the purposes

[1] Penley *vs.* City of Auburn, 85 Me., 278; Hamilton vs. City of Shelbyville, 6 Ind. App., 538.

[2] 5 Cowen, 538.

of burying their dead, it never entered into the contemplation of either party, that the health of the city might require the suspension or abolition of that right."

In the case of Crowder *vs.* Town of Sullivan,[1] the court states this principle of the inability of the city to contract with reference to its public or governmental duty by saying: "A private corporation that obtains a license to use the streets of a municipality takes it subject to the power of a municipality to enact a general ordinance; for a governmental power such as that exercised in enacting police regulations cannot be surrendered or bartered away even by express contract." Again in Snouffer *vs.* Cedar Rapids & M. C. Ry. Co.,[2] the court expresses this well established principle of law to the effect that, " in the absence of statutory authority, any contract or agreement, whether in the form of an ordinance or otherwise, which directly or indirectly surrenders or materially restricts the exercise of a governmental or legislative function or power, may at any time be terminated or annulled by the municipality."

But if the municipal corporation owns buildings and equipment and has employed men to discharge its public or governmental duties which do not require the entire service of such properties or men, it may contract for their use for private purposes.[3] The courts generally permit this diversion of forces, lawfully employed by the city for the public service, to the performance of private work under contract but only to the extent that there is a surplus of such forces. This privilege of subletting such excess properties is given by the courts in the absence of express statutory authority for the purpose of saving the loss that would result from their non-user. But authority must al-

[1] 128 Ind., 486.   [2] 92 N. W., 79.
[3] The Maggie P, 25 Fed., 202.

ways be found for the employment of these forces and the acquirement of the equipment for serving the public so that their use for private purposes is only temporary and incidental. A town, having in its public buildings rooms which it had the authority to build as a part of such structures and which are not needed for public purposes for the time being, is not obliged to let them stand idle but may realize revenue from renting them for private purposes.[1]

The case of Pikes Peak Power Co. *vs.* City of Colorado Springs,[2] offers a good statement of this rule of law, together with the reason upon which it is founded: " But it is equally true that municipalities and their officers have the power and use of all public utilities under their control for the benefit of their cities and citizens, provided always that such application does not materially impair the usefulness of these facilities for the purpose for which they were primarily created. . . . Where a city has had legislative authority to erect a dam for the purpose of providing waterworks for the city, it might lawfully lease for private purpose any excess of water not required for its waterworks. This is a just and reasonable rule. It is a rule not inconsistent with any principle of law or equity and in accord with that good sense and good business principles which recognize as a public good the growth of two blades of grass where but one grew before, and the conversion of waste to use."

Having in mind then, this distinction of the two capaci-

---

[1] French *vs.* Inhabitants of Quincy, 3 Allen, 9. The same principle was recognized in the case of George *vs.* School District, 6 Metc., 497, where the court upheld an agreement for the erection of a second story for a hall which was intended only for the occasional use of the school. To the same effect see Riverside, etc. Co. *vs.* City of Riverside, 118 Fed., 736.

[2] 105 Fed., 1.

ties in which municipal corporations may act—the one in which, as an arm of sovereignty or an agent of the state, it is charged with legislative and governmental powers; and the other in which it is a property holder and conducts a business enterprise for the private advantage of the city and its citizens, it should be remembered that this discussion is concerned chiefly with the latter division of the subject. The powers of the municipality in its former capacity are well defined and strictly limited by the statutory provisions granting them. There is little or no opportunity here for invoking the doctrine of liberal construction nor for extending its sphere of activity by the doctrine of implied powers. It is the duties of the sovereign that are to be performed in the manner provided by law and its interests alone are to be considered.

CHAPTER III

CONSTRUCTION OF MUNICIPAL CHARTERS

THE rule of law is well established to the effect that the discretion of municipal corporations, within the sphere of their powers and particularly their private powers, is not subject to judicial control, except in cases where fraud is found or where the power or discretion is being grossly abused to the oppression of the citizen.[1] In its capacity as a business organization the powers conferred on a municipal corporation are for its own special interest and advantage. The interest of the state is only secondary, and the main purpose is to benefit the particular locality incorporated and its citizens. Considering this as the chief purpose in the creation of such corporations the courts favor the exercise of the fullest discretion in carrying out the powers granted which would be consistent with the general object of the grant, and the best interests of the grantee.[2]

In the case of City of Vincennes vs. Citizens' Gas Light Co.,[3] this rule of law is laid down as follows: " The making of contracts for the supply of gas or water is a matter, delegated to the governing power of municipalities, to be exercised according to their own discretion; and in the ab-

---

[1] The City of Valparaiso vs. Gardner, 97 Ind., 1; Atlantic City Waterworks Co. vs. Atlantic City, 6 Atl., 24; Rockerbrant vs. Madison, 9 Ind. App., 227; City of St. Paul vs. Laidler, 2 Minn., 190.

[2] Sun Publishing Ass'n vs. Mayor, 152 N. Y., 257; The City of Bridgeport vs. The Housatonic Ry. Co., 15 Conn., 475.

[3] 132 Ind., 114, 126.

sence of fraud, while acting within the authority delegated to them, their action is not subject to review by the courts. The length of time for which they shall bind their towns or cities depends upon so many circumstances and conditions as to situation, cost of supply and future prospects, that the courts can interfere only in extreme cases and upon reasonable application."

In Conrey *vs.* Waterworks Co.,[1] the court said: " If the city had the power to make the contract, and confined herself within the limits of the power, the quantity and kind of water, the price, etc., were matters within the legislative discretion of the City Council, and unless there is fraud in the execution of the contract, courts will not inquire into this discretion." Again in the case of Janeway *vs.* City of Duluth,[2] the court said: " Whether or not a new water plant is necessary is a legislative question and not a judicial one. The court cannot substitute its judgment for that of the city council and the voters of the city."

The case of City of Henderson *vs.* Young,[3] also contains a good statement of this principle as well as the reason on which it is founded: " In the management and operation of its electric-light plant a city is not exercising its governmental or legislative powers, but its business powers, and may conduct it in the manner which promises the greatest benefit to the city and its inhabitants in the judgment of the city council; and it is not within the province of the court to interfere with the reasonable discretion of the council in such matters."

Finally in the case of Torrent *vs.* City of Muskegon,[4] the court in refusing to enjoin the defendant city from carrying out a contract for building a city hall, said: " But

[1] 41 La. Ann., 910.
[2] 68 N. W., 24.
[3] 83 S. W., 583.
[4] 47 Mich., 115.

in saying this, we do not assume that it belongs to this court or any other, to dictate to the city how it shall spend its money. The council must use its own discretion where it will save and where it will spend; and the case must be a very clear one, and the subterfuge very plain, before that discretion can be regarded as having been exceeded so as to show an excess of power under a pretense of keeping within it. It is not the business of courts to act as city regulators, and unless the authority of the representatives of the citizens has been exceeded, their action cannot be interfered with merely because it may not seem to other persons to be as wise as it might be."

But unless expressly authorized by statute municipal corporations have no authority to furnish entertainment for guests of the corporation at the public expense. In doing this without such authority the courts are of the opinion that there is an abuse of discretion, and that expenses are incurred which the citizens should not be made to pay. This rule is well stated in the case of Gamble *vs.* Village of Watkins.[1] This was an action to recover for meals and lodging, furnished in entertaining a party of representatives of the press, which had been authorized by a resolution of the board of trustees of said village. In refusing recovery the court said: "We think that the defendant had not power to appropriate money for the entertainment of a company of editors visiting the place. This is not a duty for which the municipality was created. It is said that the expenditure has been repaid by the effect on the village of subsequent editorial puffs. But it is not proper for village trustees to hire editors to praise the attractions of the place. If it had been shown that the editors were paupers, then, under the duty of a village to take care of

[1] 7 Hun, 448.

the poor, there might have been some propriety in keeping them from starving." Again in the case of Austin *vs.*
Coggeshall,[1] the court permanently restrained the payment
by the city treasurer of an account incurred in entertaining
officers of certain British ships of war while in Newport
harbor. "The defense would be more meritorious if the
persons in whose behalf it is interposed had any claim
on the city for value received. But they have none. The
city neither danced at the ball nor feasted at the banquet.
It got nothing substantial out of them. . . . It is well settled
that a municipal corporation, when sued directly on a contract which it is incapable of making, cannot be estopped from
taking advantage of its incapacity because the party suing
has acted on the contract in good faith."

These cases then will serve to illustrate the limitations
which the courts place on the discretion of the municipality
in cases of its abuse in order to protect the citizens. In
refusing recovery for services to the city, rendered in good
faith, the court shows how far it will go to protect the
citizens against an abuse of power by their servants, the
municipal authorities, and invokes the well accepted rule
of law which requires the individual to know the extent of
the authority possessed by the municipality in contracting
with it. And as it is axiomatic that fraud vitiates every-
thing it touches, it follows that where fraud is found the
courts will not respect the discretionary rights of municipal
corporations.[2]

With these two limitations the rule is absolute that the
discretion of municipal corporations within the sphere of

---

[1] 12 R. I., 329.

[2] City of Ft. Scott *vs.* Eads Brokerage Co., 117 Fed., 51; Waterbury
vs. City of Lorendo, 68 Tex., 365; First National Bank *vs.* Sarlls, 129
Ind., 201; Winchester *vs.* Redmond, 93 Va., 711.

their powers is as wide as that possessed by the general government. The legislative is a co-ordinate branch of government and within its sphere is supreme, and so is the municipal corporation within its prescribed limits. The judiciary has no more right to interfere with the acts of one than of the other.[1]

In construing municipal charters only such strictness is observed as gives effect to every power clearly intended to be conferred on the municipality and every power necessarily implied in order to permit of the complete exercise of the powers granted. While their sphere of activity is to be confined strictly within the limits prescribed by the law, within these limits their action is favored by our courts. And powers intended to be conferred will not be defeated or impaired by a strict construction.[2]

These principles are well expressed by the court in the case of Thomas *vs.* City of Grand Junction,[3] where it is said: " The whole spirit of the law is so far as possible to permit under reasonable restrictions the privilege of self-government. In fact, that it was the intent of the legislature in its grant of powers to municipal corporations to give them the fullest power and utmost freedom of action with reference specially and exceptionally to the securing of such a water supply as might be deemed needful, is clearly manifest from the very terms of the act."

Again in Columbus Water Co. *vs.* Mayor of Columbus,[4] the court says: " Neither would we apply the rule with the same strictness to municipal corporations that should

---

[1] 15 *American and English Encyclopædia of Law,* 1st ed., 1046 and cases cited.

[2] Smith *vs.* City of Madison, 7 Ind., 86; Kyle *vs.* Malin, 8 Ind., 34.

[3] 13 Col. App., 80.

[4] 15 L. R. A., 354.

govern private corporations organized for gain. Courts should be governed by the conditions and circumstances surrounding the municipalities, and regard them as branches of the sovereign government. When improved methods are offered which will give to the city better facilities in the way of water, light and travel or in any other manner give to its inhabitants increased safety or protection, the governing power of the city should be free to act."

Finally in Torrent *vs.* City of Muskegon,[1] the court defines the rule of construing municipal charters by saying: " If cities were new inventions, it might with some plausibility be claimed that the terms of their charters, as expressed, must be the literal and precise limits of their powers. But cities and kindred municipalities are the oldest of all existing forms of government, and every city charter must be rationally construed as intended to create a corporation which shall resemble in its essential character the class into which it is introduced. There are many flourishing cities whose charters are very short and simple documents. . . . But if we were to assume that there is nothing left to implication, we should find the longest of them too imperfect to make city action possible." [2]

[1] 47 Mich., 115.

[2] See also Baumgartner *vs.* Hasty, 100 Ind., 575; Pittsburgh, etc., Ry. Co. *vs.* The Town of Crown Point, 146 Ind., 421; The State *ex rel. vs.* City of Hiawatha, 53 Kan., 477.

CHAPTER IV

THE IMPLIED POWERS OF MUNICIPAL CORPORATIONS

THE principle of the implied powers of municipal corporations is therefore fully recognized by all our courts. Through the recognition of the existence of implied powers more than in any other way they have given effect to the purpose, and recognized the object, for which municipal corporations are established. The field is naturally a fertile one for judicial legislation and construction, and it has been freely exploited in giving effect to the powers necessary to a full enjoyment and a complete realization of the advantages of such corporations, to the end that the greatest public good might be attained. Decisions giving the most complete freedom of activity to municipalities, consistent with their best interests and not derogatory of specific statutory regulations, represent the great weight of authority. It is only a few of our courts that refuse the right of municipal corporations to keep abreast of the times and to conduct their affairs to their best advantage and for the greatest benefit of their citizens. In view of the fact that the sole purpose of such corporations in their capacity of business concerns is to benefit the people who inhabit them and thus constitute their stockholders, so to speak, it is submitted that the present advantage and the prospective advancement of these organizations should be the test of the control exercised over them by the legislature and the courts. The only other party even remotely concerned is that of the state and its interests must be identical with

those of the city.   Since the interests of the two parties involved is the same it is only reasonable to suppose that the
one party, in legislating for the other, intends always to
accomplish the greatest good for the greatest number concerned.

Because of the many details and the varying circumstances of the different cities, only general legislation with
reference to them is advisable or possible.   This necessitates the exercise of much judgment by the cities, in whose
officers must be vested a wide discretion.   And in construing such general statutes in a particular case regard
must be had for the facts and circumstances of the case in
hand so that the general law as applied will give the best
results.   It is in determining the legislative intent and in
giving such intention the most favorable application to the
particular city of which it will admit, that the courts take
the opportunity to advance the interests by extending the
scope of the activity of such municipality as its welfare requires.   And it is submitted that the authorities with very
few exceptions do favor a decided increase of the sphere
of municipal activity for the reason that the best interests
of these corporations demand it.

Under the doctrine of the implied powers of municipal
corporations the decisions of the different cases extending
their sphere of activity are based on one of three grounds.
The first which is probably the most frequently invoked
is that of the police power, whose application in this connection, as well as in others, is an excellent illustration of
the pertinent remark by one of our courts that, " it may be
said that it is known when and where it [the police power]
begins, but not when and where it terminates.[1]   Another
basis for these decisions which has been frequently given

---

[1] Champer *vs.* City of Greencastle, 138 Ind., 339.

is that of the general welfare clause found in many city charters. This is often mentioned in connection with the third reason with which it is closely allied—that the purpose is public or municipal.

All three of these are sound reasons for the decisions of our courts, recognizing in municipal corporations additional powers on the theory that they are entitled to exercise powers " necessarily or fairly implied in or incident to powers expressly granted, or those essential to the declared objects and purposes of the corporation." It may seem that the police power is the least germane and definite because of its elasticity and of the very wide application which it is given as the reason for some decisions upon almost all subjects. It is, however, a valid basis for these decisions, for the furnishing of water, light, gas, and such public utilities to the individual inhabitants of cities concerns the protection of their health, life and property, which constitutes a duty of the municipality to its citizens. But naturally the public welfare clause of the charter or the fact that the purpose is a municipal one furnishes a basis for this line of decisions that is more peculiarly applicable than that of the police power.

Statutes expressly providing that municipal corporations may furnish such public utilities as electric light, water and gas for the private use of its citizens as well as for the city are universally upheld by all our courts as constitutional.[1]

In the case of Linn *vs.* Borough of Chambersburg,[2] the court says: " The power of the legislature to authorize

---

[1] Fallows *vs.* Walker, 39 Fed., 651; Opinion of the Justices, 150 Mass., 592; Mitchell *vs.* City of Negaunee, 113 Mich., 359; Norwich Gas & Electric Co. *vs.* Norwich, 76 Conn., 565; State *ex rel. vs.* City of Toledo, 48 Ohio St., 112.

[2] 160 Pa., 511.

municipal corporations to supply gas and water for municipal purposes, and for the use and benefit of such of their inhabitants as wish to use them and are willing to pay therefor at reasonable rates, has never been seriously questioned. In view of the fact that electricity is so rapidly coming into general use for illuminating streets, public and private buildings, dwellings, etc., why should there be any doubt as to the power to authorize such corporations to manufacture and supply it in like manner as artificial gas has been manufactured and supplied? It is a mistake to assume that municipal corporations should not keep abreast with the progress and improvements of the age."

Further the power of the municipality to provide these public utilities for the private use of its citizens is implied from the power to furnish such utilities for use upon its streets and in other public places in the absence of any express legislative authority by most of our courts. There are a few decisions it is true which refuse the city the right so to extend its sphere of activity and usefulness for the advantage of its citizens. The great weight of authority, however, and certainly the better reason permits this extension of power and favors an increase of the sphere of municipal activity.

The rule of law is well established to the effect that a city, in erecting gas, water or electric-light plants, is not limited to providing the service of such utilities for use only upon the streets and in other public places of the city, but that it may in connection therewith furnish the same for the private use of its citizens. Some of our courts have even held that it is the duty of the municipality not only to light its streets and public places but to furnish its inhabitants with the means of obtaining light at their own expense.[1]

[1] City of Newport *vs.* Newport Light Co., 84 Ky., 166.

In view of this diversity of opinion of the authorities and the recent date of the decisions which make it impossible to speak of the doctrine as finally accepted by all our courts, it has been thought best to set out somewhat at length some of the decisions together with the grounds upon which they are based so that the authority may appear for the position herein taken—that our courts favor an increase of the sphere of municipal activity.

The case of Thompson Houston Electric Co. *vs.* City of Newton,[1] decided in 1890, was an action to enjoin the defendant, City of Newton, Iowa, from purchasing and operating an electric-light plant, and furnishing light for the streets and public places of said city and for the private use of its inhabitants. The only statutory authority given the city provided that it might "establish and maintain gasworks or electric-light plants, with all the necessary poles, wires, burners and other requisites of said gasworks or electric-light plants." Section 2 of the same act made the statutory authority for the erection and maintenance of gasworks and electric-light plants the same as that applicable to waterworks.[2] The court in defining the powers of the city under this statute says that: " It is also urged that the city has only the authority to erect an electric plant for the purpose of lighting the streets and public places of the city, and is not authorized to furnish lights for use in the houses and stores of its citizens. The act of the general assembly giving the right to cities to erect, or to authorize the erection of electric plants, makes no distinction between lights used for public or private purposes; and the right of the city in the erection of its own plant is not limited in any other way than is the right of a company authorized by

[1] 42 Fed.,723.
[2] Acts 22d General Assembly, Iowa, p. 16.

the city to erect the plant. It has been the uniform rule that a city, in erecting gasworks or waterworks, is not limited to furnishing gas or water for use only upon the streets and other public places of the city, but may furnish the same for private use, and the statutes of Iowa now place electric-light ·plants in the same category." This decision was cited with approval and followed in the case of State ex rel. *vs.* Allen,[1] decided in 1903, upon facts very similar to the original case. The argument advanced by the complainant that furnishing electricity to the inhabitants together with the city for public purposes was in contravention of the constitution because the purpose was not wholly a public one was not accepted by the court, which held that such power would be found in the city by implication.

The case of the City of Crawfordsville *vs.* Braden,[2] decided in 1891, is a leading one and has been frequently cited with approval. The court states the facts for decision in the question as follows: " has a municipal corporation in this State the power to erect, maintain, and operate the necessary buildings, machinery and appliances to light its streets, alleys and other public places with the electric-light, and at the same time and in connection therewith to supply electricity to its inhabitants for the lighting of their residences and places of business." The only statutory authority in point provided: " That the common council of any city in this State incorporated either under the general act for the incorporation of cities or under a special charter, and the board of trustees of all incorporated towns of this State, shall have the power to light the streets, alleys, and other public places of such city and town with the electric-light, or other form of light, and to contract with any individual or corporation for lighting such streets,

[1] 178 Mo., 555.   [2] 130 Ind., 149.

alleys, and other public places with the electric-light, or other forms of light, on such terms, and for such time, not exceeding ten years as may be agreed upon." [1]

In holding that the city might furnish electricity to its inhabitants the court said: "Among the implied powers possessed by municipal corporations is the power to enact and enforce reasonable by-laws and ordinances for the protection of health, life and property. . . . The corporation possessing, as it does, the power to generate and distribute through its limits, electricity for the lighting of its streets and other public places, we can see no good reason why it may not also, at the same time, furnish it to the inhabitants to light their residences and places of business. To do so, is in our opinion, a legitimate exercise of the police power for the preservation of property and health. It is averred in the complaint that the light which the city proposes to furnish for individual use is the incandescent light. Here again is a fact of which we are authorized to take judicial knowledge. A light thus produced is safer to property, and more conducive to health than the ordinary light. Produced by the heating of a filament of carbon to the point of incandescence in a vacuum, there is nothing to set property on fire, or to consume the oxygen in the surrounding air, and thus render it less capable of sustaining life and preserving health." The court reached its decision notwithstanding the existence of a provision in the statutes authorizing the grant to any corporation of the right to erect and maintain in the streets the necessary poles and appliances for the purpose of supplying the electric or other light to the inhabitants.

This decision is the leading one on the subject that is expressly put on the ground of the police power, and the

[1] Acts 53d General Assembly, Indiana, p. 85.

reasoning of the court in doing so has met with approval by all the decisions which accept the doctrine of implied powers in this connection. The argument of the court is convincing, and although somewhat ingenious and novel when made, is now well recognized and has been advanced in later cases following this decision. And it is submitted that this case because of its reasoning goes further than the Federal case, above mentioned, in extending the sphere of municipal activity. It will also be noted that these cases are concerned with electric-lighting which is not so essentially a matter of public health as the furnishing of a water supply or a sewerage system, and which is of course a more modern public utility.

The promptness with which our courts extended the power of municipalities to include the employment of the modern agency of electricity for private purposes, after the advantages of using it for public lighting had been demonstrated, is the best evidence that they desire to extend the sphere of usefulness of our cities whenever the opportunity is given. The courts are of the opinion that it is not only within the power of the cities but that it is their duty to keep themselves free to accept for their own use and to provide for their inhabitants new inventions and superior agencies as they arise, and that cities are not to be restricted to the providing for the strict necessities of their citizens but that they may also minister to their comfort and pleasure.[1]

The police power serves as a more natural support to the decision of the case of McBean *vs.* City of Fresno,[2] where the action was to recover the contract price for services

[1] Sun Publishing Assn. *vs.* Mayor, 8 App. Div. (N. Y.), 230; affirmed in 152 N. Y., 257.

[2] 112 Cal., 159.

rendered in disposing of sewage for the defendant city. The court said in the course of its decision that, "proper sewers are in this day so essential to the hygiene and sanitation of a municipality that a court would not look to see whether a power to construct and maintain them had been granted by the charter, but rather only to see whether, by possibility the power had been expressly denied."

And to the same effect is Ellinwood *vs.* City of Reedsburg;[1] where the court says: "It is not necessary to seek for an express delegation of power to the city to build a waterworks and electric-lighting plant in order to determine whether such power exists, for the general power in respect to police regulations, the preservation of the public health, and the general welfare includes the power to use the usual means of carrying out such powers, which includes municipal water and lighting services."

In granting the power by implication to the city to furnish its inhabitants with electric-light because such action would be for their best interests and because it would be a municipal purpose, the supreme court of Florida in Jacksonville Electric Light Co. *vs.* City of Jacksonville,[2] decided in 1895, expressed this well established principle by saying: "The grant of power to the city of Jacksonville to provide for lighting the city by gas or other illuminating material, or in any other manner, is clear and explicit, and carries with it the power of the choice of means to accomplish the end. Should this power be construed into a right to light the streets and public places of the city, but not to supply the inhabitants thereof with light for use in their private houses? . . . We are of the opinion that a fair construction of the grant 'to provide for lighting the city by gas or other illuminating material, or in any other

[1] 91 Wis., 131.   [2] 36 Fla., 229.

manner,' will authorize the erection and maintenance of an electric-light plant, not only for lighting the streets and public places of the city, but also for supplying in connection therewith, electric light for the inhabitants of the city in their private houses. The power given is to light the city, and the connection indicates that the legislature was conferring powers for the benefit of the people generally of the city. . . . That the supplying the inhabitants of a city with electric-light is such a municipal purpose as will authorize its delegation by the legislature to municipal bodies is sustained by all the authorities we have found. To the extent of supplying light to the inhabitants of a city for use in their private houses, we discover nothing that cannot, in the light of the decisions, be called a municipal purpose. . . . "

The decision in the case of Heilbron *vs.* Mayor of Cuthbert,[1] rendered in 1895, is placed expressly on the general welfare clause of the charter. The court finds that: " Under the 9th section of the charter of the City of Cuthbert (Acts of 1859, p. 149) the mayor and council of that city have authority to ' contract and be contracted with; sue and be sued; . . . and do all things for the benefit of the city, and all things not in violation of the constitution and laws of this State.' It is apparent, therefore, that the ' general welfare clause ' in this charter is very broad and liberal in its terms. That the erection and maintenance of water-works and of an electric-light plant would result in benefit to the city, is obvious. It was insisted, however, that in order to authorize a municipal corporation to contract a debt for improvements of this kind, the power to do so must be expressly conferred by the charter. We do not concur in this view." While there is no express state-

[1] 96 Ga., 312.

ment made in this case to the effect that the inhabitants
as well as the city were to be supplied with water and electricity, this would seem to have been intended, from a
remark found in connection with the statement of the
facts of the case that, " this ordinance further provides that
all revenue arising from the operation of the waterworks
and light plant should be applied first to the expenses of
their operation, etc." [1]

Among the more recent cases permitting cities to provide their citizens with electric light in their private capacity in the absence of any express legislative authority is
that of Fawcett *vs.* Mt. Airy,[2] decided in 1903.   This case
argues the question in issue at length, and indicates the
favorable attitude which is taken towards increasing the
opportunities for cities to serve their citizens with the comforts and pleasures as well as the necessities of life.   It also
shows that our courts recognize the fact that with the advance of civilization the increase of population and its con-
gestion in municipalities, making competition more keen
and living more strenuous, what were at one time regarded
as luxuries become comforts and are later looked upon as
necessities.   The case also criticises the Massachusetts court
for refusing to imply this power in municipalities to provide
its citizens with these public utilities although it had held
the purchase by them of town clocks, scales, etc., to be a
necessary expense.   Because of its importance, we quote it
at considerable length.   " Whether a city or town has the
right to incur an indebtedness for the erection and operation of plants for the supply of water and electric light for
municipal use, and to sell to its inhabitants, as a necessary
municipal expense, is the question again presented to us

[1] See also Mayor, etc., of Rome *vs.* Cabot, 28 Ga., 50.
[2] 134 N. C., 125.

for decision.   Indebtedness incurred by a city or town for
a supply of water stands on the same footing as indebtedness incurred for lighting purposes, and if such indebtedness be a necessary expense, then whether or not a municipality may incur it does not depend upon the approval of
the proposition by a majority of the qualified voters of the
municipality. . . . It is almost impossible to define, in legal
phraseology, the meaning of the words ' necessary expense,'
as applied to the wants of a city or town government.   A
precise line cannot be drawn between what are and what
are not such expenses.   The consequence is that, as municipalities grow in wealth and population, as civilization ad-
vances with the habits and customs of necessary changes,
the aid of the courts is constantly invoked to make decisions
on this subject.   In the nature of things it could not be
otherwise; and it is not to be expected, in the changed conditions which occur in the lives of progressive people, that
things deemed unnecessary in the government of municipal
corporations in one age should be so considered for all future time.   In the efforts of the courts to check extrava-
gance and to prevent corruption in the government of
towns and cities, the judicial branch of the government has
probably stood by former decisions from too conservative
a standpoint, and thereby obstructed the advance of business ideas which would be most beneficial if put into operation; and this conservatism of the courts, outgrown by the
march of progress sometimes appears at a serious disadvantage. . . . and certainly expenses incurred for water
and light are more necessary than those for a market house,
clocks, and scales.   The words ' necessary expense,' then,
must mean such expenses as are or may be incurred in
the establishing and procuring of those things without which
the peace and order of the community, its moral interests,
and the protection of its property and that of the property

and persons of its inhabitants, would seriously suffer considerable damage. . . . If the matter of lighting is a necessary expense, then how and in what manner the city shall furnish such lighting is with the authorities of the city or town to determine. . . . Our conclusion, then, is that an expense incurred by a city or town for the purpose of building and operating plants to furnish water and lights is a necessary expense. . . ." [1]

The provision of an adequate water supply for the use of the city and its inhabitants is directly concerned with its health in addition to being a municipal purpose and for the general welfare. This public utility has always been recognized as necessary for the public health and convenience and the authorities agree that it is the duty of the city to provide a water supply for protection against fire. That an adequate supply of pure water for the citizens of a large city is a necessity which can be provided only by a responsible public or quasi-public corporation is generally admitted. As compared with electricity, the question of a water supply is much older and the law, permitting cities to furnish water from their own plant to their citizens along with providing for the public wants, has become firmly established. In practice it seems to have been very generally assumed that the erection and operation of a water-works system is a municipal purpose and that the city is expected to furnish it for private use along with attending to the public demand. The courts have recognized the economy of doing this as well as the fact that it tends to the protection of health, life, and property and is therefore a legitimate exercise of the police power.[2]

---

[1] This case was followed in Greensboro *vs.* Scott, 138 N. C., 181, decided in 1905; see also Wadsworth *vs.* Concord, 133 N. C., 587.

[2] Cooley, *Taxation*, p. 217.

A good case expressing the law of this subject is that of Smith *vs.* Nashville,[1] where the only statute in point gave the mayor and city council the power " to provide the city with water by waterworks, within or beyond the boundaries of the city, and to provide for the prevention and extinguishment of fires, and to organize and establish fire companies." [2]   In the course of its well reasoned decision the court says: " It is seen at once that the waterworks are corporate property; that is not denied. The debate is with respect to the nature of the use. As to that, for the sake of convenience we divide all the purposes for which the city furnishes water into three classes: (1) to extinguish fires and sprinkle the streets; (2) to supply citizens of the city; (3) to supply persons and factories adjacent to but beyond the corporate limits.

If the business were confined to the first class, there would be no ground to base a discussion upon, so clearly would the use be exclusively for public advantage. We think there can be but little more doubt about the second class, especially in view of certain words in the city charter, to which we will advert presently. Nothing should be of greater concern to a municipal corporation than the preservation of the good health of the inhabitants; nothing can be more conducive to that end than a regular and sufficient supply of wholesome water, which common observation teaches all men can be furnished, in a populous city, only through the instrumentality of well equipped waterworks. Hence for a city to meet such a demand is to perform a public act and confer a public blessing. It is not a strictly governmental or municipal function, which every municipality is under legal obligation to assume and perform,

[1] 88 Tenn., 464.

[2] Acts 43d General Assembly, Tennessee, p. 147.

but it is very close akin to it, and should always be recognized as within the scope of its authority, unless excluded by positive law.   Here the first clause [of the statute quoted *supra*], ' to provide the city with water by waterworks ' is very broad and comprehensive, and was obviously intended to authorize the corporation to furnish the inhabitants of the city with water.   Having accepted the charter and undertaken to exercise this authority in the manner detailed by the witness, it cannot be held that the city, in doing so, is engaging in a private enterprise or performing a municipal function for a private end."

As to the power of a city to supply parties with water beyond its boundaries this Tennessee case is supplemented by that of Lawrence *vs.* Methuen [1] where an injunction to prevent this was refused.   In order to show the friendly attitude of this court toward cities as business concerns we quote from the decision as follows: " In practice it must often be a great convenience for persons owning and occupying land extending across the boundary line between two municipalities to take water from one or the other for use on the whole land; and to compel such persons to distinguish between the parts of the premises in each municipality on which the water is used, and to confine the use of the water to the part within the municipality from whose works the water is taken, would impose artificial restraints upon such owners in the use of property which could be justified only by language clearly expressing an intention to accomplish such a result, and we find no such language in St. 1892, c. 310."

These authorities, then, will serve to support the principle so far as it is based on the doctrine of implied powers that our courts, for one or more of the three valid reasons above

[1] 166 Mass., 206.

given, permit municipal corporations in connection with supplying their public wants for gas, water and electric-light services to furnish these utilities for the private use of their inhabitants. This privilege is found by implication, it is to be noted, only in case it is to be exercised in connection with supplying the public wants; and while most of our courts do not expressly give as a reason for their holdings the economy of such an arrangement, it is submitted that this is a controlling idea underlying their decisions, and expressly given in some of them.[1] This fact becomes more apparent when it is remembered that these are matters concerned with natural monopolies which render competition in practice not only inexpedient but practically impossible. This subject, however, together with the necessity for greater control in the absence of the restraints of competition will be discussed at length later.

A few courts take issue with this very reasonable principle of law which is well established by the great weight of authority and hold that, while the power to light the streets and public places of a city by electricity authorizes the erection and maintenance of a plant for that purpose, it may not be used for supplying light to private individuals. These adverse decisions are confined to the matter of furnishing electric light, which, of course, is comparatively a very modern public utility, and some of them, at least, can be distinguished from those already discussed and shown not to be actually conflicting authorities.

One of the leading cases which is apparently opposed to the principle in question is that of Mauldin *vs.* Greenville,[2] decided in 1890, in which the court granted an injunction preventing the defendant city from purchasing and operat-

[1] Belding Improvement Co. *vs.* Belding, 128 Mich., 79.
[2] 33 S. C., 1.

ing an electric-light plant, so far as it was concerned with supplying private residences. The court admits that there is no power expressly given the city to provide itself with light for public purposes. This decision, therefore, cannot be said to oppose the doctrine that where the city has the power expressly given to furnish light for city use it may as incidental to such use and in connection therewith extend the service to private parties. That is to say, in this case the statute fails to grant power in the city to furnish light for any purpose and in any way, so that the court is not passing on the question under discussion in the former cases.

In this case the court expressed itself as follows: "Clearly, the charter does not give the power to purchase this plant in express words. It does not so give even the power to light the City, but we assume that this latter power may be fairly implied from the grant of the police power. . . . This seems to be a new question. It strikes us as remarkable that, in the multitude of cases cited by the distinguished counsel who argued the case, there should not be in one of them the least reference to this precise point. We have made diligent search, and have not been able to find one. We must decide it, but without any help from authorities. The City has the express power to own property, and it also has the implied right to light the City. Do these powers necessarily imply the right to make the City the owner of the plant and a manufacturer of electricity? It is quite certain that such power is not 'essential' to the declared objects and purposes of the corporation. . . . But considering that some discretion, as to the mode and manner, should be allowed the municipality, in carrying out the conceded power to light the streets of the City, we hold that the purchase of the plant was not *ultra vires* and void, so far as it was designed to produce electricity suitable for and used in lighting the streets and public buildings of the City. But we cannot so hold as to the purchase of so much of that plant as furnished the incandescent light for use in the interior of private residences and places of business, which cannot be properly included within the power to light the streets of the City. . . . As we understand it, all the powers given to the City Council were for the sole and exclusive purpose of government, and not to enter into private business of any kind, outside of the scope of the city government."

This case, then, in refusing the right of the city to accommodate its citizens with modern lighting service for their private use was confessedly decided without the aid of authorities and at most involves the construction of powers existing by implication only to provide for public lighting. While the spirit of the case is hostile it cannot be said to be an authority in conflict with the line of decisions above discussed, for they involve the extension of the authority expressly given the city to provide these public utilities for its own wants, and together therewith those of its citizens who desire to avail themselves of the opportunity and are willing to pay therefor. It is further submitted that the decision is not sound and that the court was in error in saying that " all the powers given to the City Council were for the sole and exclusive purpose of government." There can be no question under the law that the powers of municipalities are much broader than this, as common observation shows must be the case in practice.

In referring to this case the court of Nebraska in Christensen *vs.* City of Fremont,[1] decided in 1895, said, " that while the power to light the streets authorizes the erection and maintenance of a plant for lighting the streets, it does

[1] 45 Neb., 160.

not authorize one for supplying light to private buildings."
The court then goes on to admit that " the act of 1889. . .
extends the grant of power to the purpose in question,"
saying: " We have, thus, elaborated on the grant of powers
because the conclusions reached convince us that in the
absence of the act of 1889 the city could not have devoted
any revenue to the purpose of maintaining a plant to furnish light for private consumers." This case, then, is
not an authority in conflict with the principle under discussion for the reason that the decision was made six years
after the passage of an act expressly permitting the city
to serve its inhabitants with electric light, which act was
recognized by the decision as having this effect on the case.
These expressions of the court on the subject are mere
dicta, having no force of law whatever and were not necessary or proper in the decision, for they are directly contrary
to what the court admits to be the law.

In the case of Spaulding *vs.* Town of Peabody,[1] the
court denies the defendant the right to furnish light to
its inhabitants in the absence of any express statutory
power in connection with supplying the streets and public
places of the city. The court in this case fails to follow
its earlier decisions holding that the providing of clocks,
scales and the like is a public purpose and within the inherent power of cities. It can hardly be successfully maintained that the supply of light and heat by the municipality
for the private wants of citizens in connection with its plant
for supplying the public needs is any less a public purpose
than the providing of town clocks, scales, and pumps, nor
that the convenience and comfort of its citizens would require the one and not the other. In fact, experience shows
that in crowded city life electric light and gas as well as a

[1] 153 Mass., 129.

wholesome supply of water in private houses and places of business are practically necessities, and there can be no doubt that the adequate supply of such public utilities tends very materially to the preservation of public health and peace and to the protection of property. This court had found that the supply of water by a waterworks system is a public purpose and also had conceded that the Legislature has unquestioned power to permit cities to provide gas or electric-light for the private use of its citizens.[1]

In refusing to find such power by implication the court says: " It is wholly for the Legislature to determine, within the limitations of the Constitution, the powers which towns shall possess, and when it appears that the custom of the Legislature has been specifically to define from time to time the purposes for which towns may raise money by the taxation of their inhabitants, and when the Legislature can at any time grant additional powers if they are deemed necessary, a somewhat strict construction of existing statutes seems reasonable, and in accordance with the presumed intention of the Legislature. . . . The subject of constructing and maintaining gas or electric works for the manufacture of gas or electricity and the distribution thereof through the streets of towns and cities, for the purpose of furnishing light is one of too much importance to be attached as a mere incident to the power given to erect and maintain street lamps, and we think that if the Legislature had intended that towns generally should have authority to erect and maintain such works, the authority would have been plainly expressed in the statutes. . . . . "

In connection with this clearly defined position of the Massachusetts court it should be said that the towns of

[1] Opinion of the Justices, 150 Mass., 592.

New England are peculiar in that power must be given them expressly and that money can be raised by taxation only for purposes expressed in the statute or incidental to such purposes.[1] With this in mind it will be seen that the case just mentioned is not applicable to, or binding on, our courts generally for an examination of our city charters will disclose no attempt at such detailed legislation as was found binding on this particular court.

It is of interest to note that after this decision was handed down, January 12, 1891, the Legislature promptly acted upon the suggestion made in the case, and passed a general act, which was approved June 4, 1891, giving any city or town the power to construct, purchase or lease, and maintain within its limits one or more plants for the manufacture and distribution of gas or electricity for furnishing light for the municipal use, or light, heat or power, except for the operation of electric cars, for the use of its inhabitants.[2] This act was passed pursuant to the Opinion of the Justices,[3] rendered May 27, 1890, in which the court, in response to the question propounded to it by the Legislature, stated that it was within the province of that body to confer upon towns and cities the power to manufacture and distribute gas or electricity for the use of their inhabitants.

The appellate court of Illinois in Village of Ladd *vs.* Jones,[4] decided in 1895, in refusing recovery for electric lighting furnished under an ordinance by the plaintiff city to one of its inhabitants for private use, took the position that such city acted without authority in furnishing such light because such power had not been expressly granted

[1] Dillon, *Municipal Corporations*, sec. 30.
[2] Statutes, Massachusetts, 1891, c. 370.
[3] 150 Mass., 592.   [4] 61 Ill. App., 584.

to it, and expressed itself to the effect that, " powers granted to cities and villages by Legislative grant must be strictly construed." It is to be regretted that the case is not discussed more at length so that the reason for the decision might more clearly appear, and also that this question has not been passed upon by the supreme court of the State. In the case of Blanchard *vs.* Village of Benton,[1] this same court in 1903 indicates that it is still of the opinion expressed in the former case.

The Supreme Court of New Jersey in Howell *vs.* Millville,[2] decided in 1896, even denies that an act " authorizing the lighting of public streets, and places in the cities, towns, townships, boroughs, and villages of the State and to erect and maintain the proper appliances, etc.," gives the power to a municipality to erect and maintain an electric-light plant to light its streets. It is submitted that in view of this express statute the case in refusing to find authority for the city to erect and maintain an electric-light plant, for supplying the public wants, is unsound in its reasoning and so narrow in its construction as not only to fail to give effect to the intention of the legislature, but virtually to annul the enactment. The case is unsupported by authorities and does not represent the attitude of our courts outside of the particular jurisdiction.

Finally a California case decided in February, 1906, Hyatt *vs.* Williams,[3] also refuses to accept the doctrine of implied powers in this connection. It says: " The terms of the express grant of the power to provide light for the public purposes named do not indicate any intention to give the distinct and larger power to establish a plan for furnishing light for private use to all the inhabitants of the city who

[1] 109 Ill. App., 569.   [2] 60 N. J. L., 95.
[3] 84 Pac., 41.

may desire it, and no such intention can be imputed to the framers of the charter from the language there employed. . . . The question whether or not, if the city had erected or should erect a plant to supply electric light for the public streets, public places, and public buildings, it would have power to distribute any surplus thereof to the inhabitants for private use does not arise in the case." In the course of this rather arbitrary decision the court unfortunately speaks only very briefly of the reasons for holding that the power of the municipality must be so limited; and no case is discussed or even cited and no authority whatever is referred to except the general definition of the powers of municipal corporations formulated by Judge Dillon over forty years before and probably twenty years before electricity was thought of for lighting purposes as it is now enjoyed.

CHAPTER V

WHAT ARE MUNICIPAL PURPOSES WITHIN THE MEANING OF THE CONSTITUTION

THE attitude of our courts in their construction of constitutional limitations on powers vested in cities by statutory enactment when such authority is attacked on the theory that the expenditure of money in carrying out such powers would be illegal and beyond the powers of municipalities also favors an increase of the sphere of municipal activity. This line of decisions is not concerned with the doctrine of the implied powers of municipal corporations but with construing their statutory powers within the meaning of the Constitution in order to determine what are municipal purposes for the support of which the people may be required to pay by taxation. Although any abuse of authority which causes the imposition of taxation without right has been jealously guarded against by our courts as a violation of one of the very first and most fundamental of principles since the day of Magna Charta, it is submitted the authorities show that our courts have been very liberal in extending the meaning of the term, "municipal purpose," so as to permit our cities promptly to take advantage of new inventions and modern conveniences for their inhabitants.

The case of Hequembourg *vs*. City of Dunkirk,[1] decided in 1888, was an action to enjoin the defendant city from constructing an electric-light plant. The question decided by this case is whether the issuing of bonds to establish an

[1] 49 Hun, 550.

electric-light system for the purpose of supplying the said
city and its inhabitants with electricity is in violation of
article 8, section 11 of the Constitution, which provides
that " no county, city, town or village shall hereafter give
any money, . . . nor shall any such county, city, town or
village be allowed to incur any indebtedness, except for
county, city, town or village purposes." In refusing to
enjoin the erection of the plant the court held that furnishing electricity for the private use of the citizens was the
performance of a municipal purpose when done in connection with the ownership and operation of the plant for supplying the public needs of the city, saying in part: " We
think it may safely be assumed that the lighting of the
streets and public places is one of the duties devolving upon
the municipal government, and is a city purpose within the
provisions of the Constitution. What is and what is not
a municipal purpose is, in many cases, doubtful and un-
certain, and it is the duty of the courts in such cases to
give weight to the legislative determination and not to
annul its acts, unless it clearly appears that the act was
not authorized. . . . If we are correct in this view, we fail
to see why gas or electric light works may not be sanctioned
on the same theory. The lighting of the streets by gas
involves the necessity of laying mains through the streets,
with which the lamps may be supplied with gas; and, in
lighting by electricity, the stringing of wires or the laying
of conduits, through which the electricity may be conveyed.
Light in dwellings is as important and essential as upon the
streets, and promotes the general comfort, safety and welfare of the inhabitants; and when it is supplied in connection with that which is furnished by the municipality, under its duty to the public, we think it may be regarded as
an incident thereto, and one of the purposes for which the
municipality may properly contract."

The case of The People ex rel. Murphy *vs.* Kelly,[1] decided in 1879, is a leading one and indicates the liberal policy of the courts in this connection to be one of long standing. In the course of its decision, finding that the cities concerned had the power to erect the Brooklyn bridge, the court said: " Having nothing to say about the wisdom of the legislation under consideration, I am confident in the conclusion that the construction of this bridge is a city purpose of each city, and that each city can incur debt for the same, and that the act of 1875 is not in conflict with any provisions of the constitution."

The case of Sun Publishing Ass'n. *vs.* Mayor,[2] is of special interest as showing the attitude of the court with reference to the increasing and elastic powers belonging to municipal corporations. The court defined its position on the question clearly and frankly as follows: " The question is then raised whether a rapid transit railroad, wholly within the limits of a city, is a city purpose. . . . In considering this question it must be premised that cities are not limited to providing for the strict necessities of their citizens. Under legislative authority, they may minister to their comfort, health, pleasure, or education. . . . To hold that the Legislature of this State, acting as the *parens patriae*, may employ for the relief or welfare of the inhabitants of the cities of the State only those methods and agencies which have proved adequate in the past would be a narrow and dangerous interpretation to put upon the fundamental law. No such interpretation has thus far been placed upon the organic law by the courts of this State. Whenever the question has been considered, it has been universally treated in the broadest spirit. . . . The true

[1] 76 N. Y., 475.
[2] 8 App. Div. (N. Y.), 230; affirmed 152 N. Y., 257.

test is that which requires that the work shall be essentially public and for the general good of all the inhabitants of the city. It must not be undertaken merely for gain or for private objects. Gain or loss may incidentally follow, but the purpose must be primarily to satisfy the need or contribute to the convenience of the people of the city at large. Within that sphere of action, novelty should impose no veto. Should some inventive genius by and by create a system for supplying us with pure air, will the representatives of the people be powerless to utilize it in the great cities of the State, however extreme the want and dangerous the delay? Will it then be said that pure air is not so important as pure water and clear light? We apprehend not."

The New York Supreme Court reiterated in 1900 its favorable attitude toward the increase of the sphere of municipal activity in the case of Parsons *vs.* Van Wyck.[1] In this case it refused relief on an action brought by a taxpayer to restrain an alleged unlawful expenditure of municipal funds by the defendants, who were members of the Soldiers' and Sailors' Memorial Arch Commission of the City of New York provided for by chapter 522 of the Laws of 1893, and were engaged in erecting a proposed memorial monument in Riverside Park near Eighty-ninth Street. The court stated its decision after referring to other similar cases by saying, " In the same liberal spirit, we think the erection of a beautiful monument or memorial is serving a public purpose."

In the case of Townsend *vs.* City of Boston,[2] decided in 1905, the Supreme Court of Massachusetts recognized and held to be valid a statute under which the city of Boston owned and operated a certain ferry. The case was

[1] 56 App. Div. (N. Y.), 329.   [2] 187 Mass., 283.

an action in tort for personal injuries sustained by the plaintiff to the action while a passenger on a ferry boat which the defendant city owned and was operating.

In the Opinion of the Justices,[1] as given in 1890, in reply to certain questions submitted to the court by the Legislature, it is held that, if the Legislature be of the opinion that the general welfare and convenience of the inhabitants of municipalities will be promoted by giving the cities the power of furnishing them with gas or electricity for light, such power may be so conferred within the Constitution. In the course of its opinion the court said that: " The statutes are well known which authorize cities and towns to maintain waterworks for supplying their inhabitants with water, and the constitutionality of these statutes has not been doubted." The court defines the limitation to be placed on this power in Opinion of the Justices,[2] in refusing the right of the Legislature within the Constitution to confer on municipalities the power to purchase and to furnish coal and wood for fuel to its inhabitants because the carrying on of such a business for the public benefit could not be regarded as a public or municipal service.

The case of Middleton *vs.* St. Augustine,[3] decided in 1900, holds that under the Constitution of that State the Legislature can authorize municipal corporations to erect and own electric-light plants for supplying lights to their citizens and to issue bonds for such purpose, either with or without the sanction of its individual citizens or taxpayers because the purpose is municipal. To the same effect is the case of Greensboro *vs.* Scott,[4] decided in 1905. In this case the court held valid the issue of bonds to provide a municipality with a waterworks plant, a sewerage

[1] 150 Mass., 592.
[2] 155 Mass., 598.
[3] 42 Fla., 287.
[4] 138 N. C., 181.

system and for the grading and paving of its streets. The
case of Newport *vs.* Unity,[1] which was decided in 1896,
holds to this same rule of law for that State. In the
case of State ex rel. *vs.* Allen,[2] decided in 1903, the power
by virtue of statutory enactment is recognized in the city
to own and operate an electric plant for the use of the
city and its inhabitants because its purpose is public. The
case of Hazlehurst *vs.* Mayes,[3] in 1904 decided this to be
the law in the state of Mississippi.

The case of Mealy *vs.* Hagerstown,[4] decided in 1901,
states this well established rule of law as follows: " It
[the defendant city] is certainly authorized to provide for
lighting the streets and other public places within the corporate limits. We do not understand it to be seriously
questioned that it can furnish light to its citizens, if the
act of 1900 is valid. There are many cases which establish
the right of a municipality, owning its plant for lighting,
to provide light to its citizens just as it may supply them
with water, if the legislature so authorizes."

The case of State ex rel. *vs.* City of Toledo,[5] decided in
1891, is of special interest because it refused to enjoin the
defendant city from supplying natural gas for its public use
and the private use of its inhabitants. The very clear and
common-sense reasoning of the court follows: " Taxation
implies an imposition for a public use. . . . But what are
public purposes is a question that must be left to the legislature, to be decided upon its own judgment and discretion.
Water, light and heat are objects of prime necessity. Their
use is general and universal. It is now well settled that
the legislature in the exercise of its constitutional power

[1] 68 N. H., 587.   [2] 178 Mo., 555.
[3] 84 Miss., 7.   [4] 92 Md., 741.
[5] 48 Ohio St., 112.

may authorize cities to approprate real estate for water-works, etc. What we have said in reference to waterworks is for the most part applicable to the erecting and main-taining of natural or artificial gas works. Heat being an agent or principle indispensable to the health, comfort and convenience of every inhabitant of our cities, we do not see why through the medium of natural gas, it may not be as much a public service to furnish it to the citizens as to furnish water. It is sufficient if every inhabitant who is so situated that he can use it, has the same right to use it as the other inhabitants. The establishmment of natural gas-works by municipal corporations, with the imposition of taxes to pay the cost thereof, may be a new object of muni-cipal policy; but in deciding whether in a given case the object for which taxes are assessed is a public or a private purpose, we cannot leave out of view the progress of so-ciety, the change of manners and customs and the develop-ment and growth of new wants, natural and artificial, which may from time to time call for a new exercise of legislative power; and in deciding whether such taxes shall be levied for the new purposes that have arisen we should not, we think, be bound by an inexorable rule that would embrace only those objects for which taxes have been customarily and by long course of legislation levied."   The validity of this Ohio Statute giving municipal corporations the power to supply their inhabitants with gas was sustained by the Supreme Court of the United States, in the case of Hamil-ton Gaslight & Coke Co. *vs.* Hamilton City.[1]

Finally Judge Cooley in his excellent work on Taxation at p. 217, says: " The propriety and necessity of provi-sion by taxation for a supply of water for the extinguish-ment of fires, and for the general use of the inhabitants of

[1] 146 U. S., 258.

large towns, is not disputed. . . . Cities may also be authorized to construct gasworks in order to furnish their citizens with light as well as to supply the corporate needs. . . . " The principle laid down by the cases above referred to and others, is stated in 10 American and English Encyclopaedia of Law, p. 865, as follows: " It is generally agreed that the legislature has the power to authorize a municipality to own and operate an electric-light plant which shall furnish not only the lights needed by the municipality for lighting the streets and public places, but lights to the inhabitants for their private purposes." [1]

[1] See also the cases of Mitchell *vs.* City of Negaunee, 113 Mich., 359; Linn *vs.* Borough of Chambersburg, 160 Pa., 511; Levis *vs.* City of Newton, 75 Fed., 884; Norwich Gas and Electric Co. *vs.* Norwich, 76 Conn., 565.

CHAPTER VI

EXEMPTION FROM TAXATION OF MUNICIPAL PROPERTY USED FOR SUPPLYING PUBLIC UTILITIES

THE facility with which a municipal corporation may increase its sphere of activity by assuming the operation of public utilities is largely affected by the attitude of the government towards the property devoted to these purposes as expressed in the law with regard to their taxation. For even where taxes are imposed with the single idea of securing revenue, which of course is usually the case, a municipality whose waterworks or other public utilities owned and operated by it are not subject to either federal, state, or local taxation can perform the desired service much more easily than it could were such property subject to taxation. The attitude of the courts with regard to the taxation of municipal property has therefore an important bearing on the subject under consideration.

This subject may be treated from the point of view of constitutional power and from that of judicial construction of existing statutes. Since the decision of the United States Supreme Court in the case of South Carolina *vs.* United States,[1] it must be accepted as the law that the United States government has the power to tax all business undertakings of municipal corporations. In this case it was held that the state dispensaries for the sale of liquor were subject to the tax imposed by the law of Congress taxing the sale of liquor.

[1] 199 U. S., 437.

There is also no doubt as to the power of the states under the ordinary state constitutions to tax the property of municipal corporations. But generally such constitutional provisions do not require the taxation of even what is regarded as the private property of municipal corporations. The court of Kentucky however has taken the other view of the constitution of that state.[1]

When we consider the law as laid down by the courts in the absence of pertinent constitutional provision, we must distinguish between the property of municipal corporations which is used for a distinctly governmental purpose and that which is used in connection with the operation by such corporations of a municipal public utility.

The rule of law is universally accepted by all our courts to the effect that public property and the instrumentalities of government, whether pertaining to the federal, state, or municipal government, which are held for public or governmental purposes, are not, in the absence of a statute to that effect, subject to taxation. Although this immunity from taxation is generally confirmed expressly by constitutional provisions or statutory grants it is based on one of the most fundamental principles of government and good business methods and, in the absence of any express provision, is implied by our courts from the necessity of preventing the functions and activities of government from being interfered with or impeded. This principle is strictly adhered to for the further practical purpose of avoiding the useless and inconsistent formality of permitting the government to tax itself to pay itself money which could only be finally secured by other taxation.[2] It is evident that no benefit could accrue from such a proceeding except to

[1] Clark *vs.* Louisville Water Co., 90 Ky., 515.

[2] People *ex rel. vs.* Assessor of City of Brooklyn, 111 N. Y., 505.

the taxing officers whose compensation would simply add so much more to the net amount necessary to be raised for the support of the government.[1]

While the authorities are uniform in exempting from taxation by implication property held and used by the municipality for public and governmental purposes, all the courts cannot be said to be of the opinion that property of municipal corporations which is used by them in their private business capacity in furnishing such public utilities as gas, water and electric light is entitled to such exemption. In fact as has been said the court of one jurisdiction has held a statute expressly exempting such property from taxation to be unconstitutional.[2]

It is submitted, however, that, if within the meaning of the constitution, the provision of these utilities is a public purpose and the property so used is devoted to a public trust, for the acquisition of which money may be raised by taxation because the purpose is a public or municipal one, the property so acquired and used should be entitled to exemption from taxation the same as other city property. As a matter of reason if the purpose is such a municipal one that these plants of the city providing public utilities may be acquired and maintained by taxation, it remains public or municipal from the point of view of the law of taxation; and as a practical business principle the taxing of such property which is acquired and maintained wholly at the public expense by taxation, except as some revenue may be derived from its use and operation, is simply taxing the property of the city for its own support with the necessary result that nothing of any net value to the city is acquired to offset the expense of such taxation.

[1] Cooley, *Taxation*, p. 263.
[2] Clark *vs.* Louisville Water Co., 90 Ky., 515.

Nor should the fact that revenue may be derived from the operation of such plants by the city change the principle of their exemption from taxation, for in no sense can that fact alter the nature of the use to which such property is put nor the purpose accomplished by such use. And this is the test of its being a proper subject of support by taxation and of exemption from taxation. That revenue may be realized from such plants, tending to make them self-supporting, is no reason for subjecting them to the payment by taxation for their own support and that of the government to which they belong. This incidental matter of revenue does not change the nature of the use or purpose of such property from a public governmental one to one that is private and conducted for the sole purpose of pecuniary profit and so liable to taxation, as is contended in some of the cases to which reference will be made.

That public property yielding revenue is not a proper subject for taxation on that account is well illustrated in the case of People ex rel. *vs.* Assessor of City of Brooklyn,[1] where the court passed upon the matter of the right of the defendant city to tax property within its limits belonging to the city of New York and used by such city for a landing-place for its ferry which was being operated between the two cities. The reasoning of the court in refusing such right of taxation follows: " We think the landing-place was not taxable, upon the principle that property used for public purposes, is not a taxable subject, within the purview of the tax laws, unless specially included. . . . There would be manifest incongruity in subjecting to taxation for public purposes property dedicated to or acquired under legislative authority for public and governmental use. . . . . The fact that the city of New York operates the ferry

[1] 111 N. Y., 505.

through lessees, and derives its revenue from the rental, and not from the operation of the ferry by its immediate agents and servants does not make the franchise or the landing taxable. . . . The tax is imposed on the land as the property of the city, and not on the lessees in respect of their interest."

To this same effect is the case of City of Somerville *vs.* City of Waltham,[1] which is of interest for the further reason that it assists in defining the scope of the term "municipal purpose" in connection with this matter of taxation. The court said, "There is nothing in our statutes to prevent a city or town from acquiring by purchase land in another city or town for municipal purposes, if it is necessary or expedient for the interests of its inhabitants to do so. . . . While there is no specific exemption from taxation in Pub. st. c. 11, sec. 5, of the property of counties or municipal corporations, yet it is well settled that such property, when appropriated to public uses, is exempt from taxation. . . . As the land in question was purchased for the purpose of obtaining therefrom gravel for the construction and repair of streets in the plaintiff city, and has since been used for that purpose, we have no doubt that it is appropriated to public use, and is exempt from taxation."

But that property which had been purchased for the purpose of some time being used for enlarging the jail in a certain town, but which had not been actually appropriated to that purpose but was being rented to private parties, will not be held exempt from taxation by implication, because it was not devoted to a public use, was held in the case of Inhabitants of County of Essex *vs.* City of Salem.[2] In this case the court stated this limitation on the general principle as follows: "We are of the opinion that, in the

[1] 170 Mass., 160.   [2] 153 Mass., 141.

absence of any express exemption of the property of counties from taxation, an exemption can be implied only when the property is actually appropriated to public use."

With reference specially to the matter of the exemption from taxation of municipal property devoted to the supplying of such public utilities as gas, water and electric light for the city and its citizens the following cases are given to illustrate the principle of law involved. The case of Wayland *vs.* County Commissioners,[1] in 1855, decided that lands taken by the city of Boston under an act [2] for supplying that city with water were not liable to taxation within such city. The court indicated its position by saying: " Regarding this land as taken and holden for the public use, and the buildings erected upon it as necessarily incident to such use, they are both to be held public works, and as such exempted from taxation. . . . It can only be on the ground that this land was taken for public uses, that the exercise of the right of eminent domain by the government can be justified. . . . It would be difficult, we think, to find any class of cases in which the right of eminent domain is more justly or wisely exercised than in provisions to supply our crowded towns and cities with pure water—provisions equally necessary to the health and safety of the people."

This principle, which is firmly established in the law and good sense and good business principles, was clearly enunciated by the court of New York in 1880 in the case of Rochester *vs.* Town of Rush,[3] as follows: " The property assessed forms a part of a system of waterworks, imposed upon the city of Rochester by direct legislative enactment . . . for the use of its inhabitants, and the extinguishment of fires . . . and the work undertaken in pursuance of its

[1] 4 Gray, 500.   [2] Statutes, Massachusetts, 1846, c. 167.
[3] 80 N. Y., 302.

directions must be regarded as executed for the public good, and the property therefore held for public purposes. It is itself the result or product of taxation. It stands in the place of the money so raised, and therefore cannot be taken or diminished by taxation. This is clearly so upon principle, but it is also well settled by authority. . . . I am unable to perceive that in any sense the waterworks can be regarded as the private property of the city as distinguished from property held by it for public use. These considerations lead to the opinion that the property was not taxable, and that the proceedings on the part of the assessors of the town of Rush, in regard thereto, cannot be sustained."

This case represents the great weight of the authority on this subject and its reasoning has commended itself to almost all our courts. In so far, however, as the court refused the right of one municipality to tax the property of another within its limits although devoted to such a public use as the furnishing of water to its inhabitants, the law of this jurisdiction has been changed expressly by statute as appears from the case of People ex rel. *vs.* Hess,[1] which decided in 1898 that the property belonging to the waterworks system of the relator, the city of Amsterdam, located in the town of Perth was subject to taxation. The court explains its decision by saying: " It is conceded that prior to this statute,[2] the property assessed was not liable to taxation, as it was held by a municipal corporation for public use. This exemption rested on no statutory provision, but upon a principle of the common law supported by numerous cases in England and this country. We are of the opinion the Tax Law of 1896 has changed this rule and that property held by a municipal corporation for public use,

[1] 157 N. Y., 42.   [2] Chapter 908 of the Laws of 1896.

but located beyond the boundaries of the municipality is subject to general taxation."

This limitation on the immunity from taxation of municipal waterworks property as made expressly by statute was fully accepted as binding on the court. The right of the legislature to tax such property of the municipality has not been doubted, although the expediency of doing so for the general purposes of taxation may be open to question. Where a large portion of such property is within the limits of another town or city the courts, under statutory provision for doing so, concede that the latter taxing district is entitled to revenue from such property in the form of taxes and the cases of Newport *vs.* Unity,[1] and Miller *vs.* Fitchburg,[2] so hold. This same limitation would seem to have been intended by the statute of New Jersey and accepted by the court in its decision of this question in State, Water Commissioners of Jersey City *vs.* Gaffney.[3] The statute in question provided that, "All real estate belonging to the mayor and common council of Jersey City, and held within the county of Hudson for purposes connected with the works for supplying said city with water shall hereafter be exempt from taxation." In holding such property within said county not liable for taxation the court said, " it is true that the property was not in actual use when the assessment was made, but there was then no indication of any abandonment of the purpose to use it for a reservoir; on the contrary, it is clear that it was held for that necessary purpose, and without being used for any other."

The general exemption of such property without any limitation as to location was allowed as early as 1877 in the case of Town of West Hartford *vs.* Board of Water Com-

[1] 68 N. H., 587.   [2] 180 Mass., 32.
[3] 34 N. J. L., 131.

missioners,[1] and this rule seems to prevail still in the particular jurisdiction. The action arose out of an attempt on the part of the plaintiff municipality to tax that part of the waterworks property of the City of Hartford which was within the territory of the former city. In refusing this right the court said: " The [defendant] Board of Water Commissioners were authorized by the legislature to purchase and hold land in the town of West Hartford for the purpose of storing and carrying it thence to the city of Hartford for the use of its inhabitants. . . . Money in the keeping of a municipality as the result of the exercise of its power of taxation, for one public use, is not to be made to pay tribute to another public use. It has ceased to be taxable property in any legislative or judicial sense. The introduction of a supply of water for the preservation of the health of its inhabitants by the city of Hartford is unquestionably . . . for the public good in the judicial sense of that term; not indeed as the discharge of one of the few governmental duties imposed upon it, but as ranking next in order. . . . Besides the fact that rents at the present time are sufficient to pay the annual charges may be only a fortunate occurrence; this state of things may not continue [and does not make its property subject to taxation]."

The same principle was established by the court of Ohio in 1894 in the case of the City of Toledo *vs.* Yeager,[2] as applied to a municipal gas plant. The Constitution of that State provided that, " public property used exclusively for any public purpose may by general laws be exempted from taxation." After finding the use of this property to be public on the authority of the decision of the case of State ex rel. *vs.* City of Toledo,[3] the court held that under the

---

[1] 44 Conn., 360.   [2] 8 Ohio Cir. Ct. Rep., 318.   [3] 48 Ohio St., 112.

authority of this case the legislature had the authority to exempt this property from taxation and that it had done so. The court concluded its decision by saying: " The evidence shows this property to be devoted to the very purposes which are named in the statute, and which the Supreme Court has declared to be public purposes."

In 1903 this principle of exemption was clearly and fully enunciated by the court of Kansas in the case of Sumner Co. *vs.* Wellington,[1] where the following language was used: " The supplying of water to the inhabitants while not strictly a governmental function so much affects the health and welfare of the people as to be closely akin to it. . . . The ownership and the purpose being public, there are good reasons why the property should be exempted from taxation. . . . The Statute makes public ownership of property the ground of immunity from taxation, and as the plant in question is absolutely owned by the city, it is strictly within the terms of that exemption. The fact that, in establishing and carrying on a system of waterworks, the city furnishes water to citizens and consumers for rental charges, does not make it a mere business enterprise nor does it affect the exemption. The earnings derived from the water furnished for domestic use and to consumers is, as we have seen, paid into the city treasury, and used in carrying on the city government and thus inures to the benefit of the people of the municipality."

To the same effect is the case of Smith *vs.* Nashville,[2] where the court in upholding the exemption of the property of the municipal waterworks from taxation said: " To provide the city with waterworks is very broad and comprehensive and was obviously intended to authorize the corporation to furnish the inhabitants of the city with water. Having

---

[1] 66 Kan., 590.   [2] 88 Tenn., 464.

accepted the charter, and undertaken to exercise this authority in the matter detailed by the witness, it cannot be held
that the city in doing so is engaging in a private enterprise,
or performing a municipal function for a private end. It
is the use of corporate property for corporate purposes in
the sense of the Revenue Law of 1877. It can make no
difference whether the water be furnished the inhabitants
as a gratuity or for a recompense, the sum raised in the
latter case being reasonable and applied for legitimate purposes. So raising a fund to help defray the expense of
operating the waterworks, and to keep down the interest
of the City's indebtedness, incurred in the construction
thereof, is no more engaging in business for gain and profit than would be the assessment and collection of taxes for
that or any other legitimate object. To the extent that
money is realized by sale of water, if it be so termed, the
necessity of laying taxes in the usual way is diminished."

This sound legal and business principle exempting from
taxation municipal property devoted to the public use of
supplying the city and its inhabitants with the public utilities of gas and water is denied application and refuted as
unsound by the court of Kentucky. The case of City of
Louisville *vs.* Commonwealth,[1] decided in 1864, shows the
attitude of that court to be a peculiar one, and the law of
that case still obtains in this jurisdiction. In the course
of its decision on this subject of tax exemption the court
defined its position by saying: " Whatever property, such
as court-houses, prisons, and the like, which becomes necessary or useful to the administration of the municipal government, and is devoted to that use, is exempt from state
taxation: but whatever is not so used, but is owned and
used by Louisville in its social or commercial capacity as

[1] 62 Ky., 295.

a private corporation, and for its own profit, such as vacant
lots, market houses, fire engines, and the like is subject
to taxation."

That this cannot be the law is beyond question and the
application of such a rule might result in the total destruction of cities by doing away with their fire departments in
permitting their sale for non-payment of taxes. The position of this court cannot be defended from the standpoint
of law or reason and its practical application would be
highly dangerous. Speaking of this decision, Judge Cooley
in his excellent work on Taxation says:[1] "but this, unless
confined to the case of special assessments, would seem to
be limiting the implied exemption unreasonably, and certainly more than other cases limit it."

This same court in 1890 in the case of Clark *vs.* Louisville Water Co.,[2] held to be unconstitutional a statute of
that state exempting from taxation all of the property of
the defendant company, the entire stock of which was
owned by the city of Louisville. The court found that,
"the first section of our Bill of Rights provided that 'no
man or set of men are entitled to exclusive, separate public
emoluments or privileges from the community but in consideration of public service.'" We think it evident that the
furnishing of water by the company to the city for fire protection free of charge was not what induced the passage of
the act. . . . The reason which induced the attempted
granting of the exemption must, therefore, have been, as
indeed the act recites, that the sinking fund of the city, or
in other words the city itself, owned all the water company
stock. The question, therefore is, did the fact that the
sinking fund, or in other words the city, owned the water
company stock, constitute a valid consideration for the ex-

[1] Page 267.   [2] 90 Ky., 515.

emption? A municipal corporation has a double character. In one it acts strictly in its governmental capacity. In the other for the profit or convenience of its citizens. Considered in the latter light it occupies the attitude of a private corporation merely, while in the former it is an arm of the state government or a part of its political power. . . . The property necessary to the exercise of those duties which are strictly governmental is exempt from taxation, but this is not so of that which is held by the municipality for the comfort of its citizens, individually or collectively, or for money-making purposes merely. . . . The fact that the furnishing of water may incidentally protect from fire the public buildings of the state will not support the exemption."

The law of this case is followed and extended to a general application of this rule denying the right of exemption to such property in the case of Covington *vs.* Commonwealth,[1] decided in 1897.[2] It should be noted, however, that this court in City of Covington *vs.* District of Highlands,[3] in following the law enunciated in the Clark case, *supra,* denied the right to sell the municipal waterworks property for non-payment of taxes assessed against it; but provided in case of failure to make such payment, a receiver for the property might be appointed to collect funds with which to make such payment. While this may indicate the desire of this court to show some consideration for the preservation of the integrity of such a system, in the interest of the public which is absolutely dependent upon its continued operation, it is submitted that the effect of a receiver in the great majority of cases would be fatal to the successful

---

[1] 107 Ky., 680.

[2] This decision was affirmed in 1900 in Negley *vs.* City of Henderson, 22 Ky. L. R., 912.

[3] 113 Ky., 612.

continuation of such a system, and would result in its
final dissolution and destruction.

The court of Pennsylvania as early as 1880 in the case
of Chadwick *vs.* Maginnes,[1] denied the right of a municipal
waterworks plant to exemption from taxation under a
statute subjecting to taxation all property not expressly
exempt, and especially property from which any income or
revenue is derived. In this decision the court found that:
" While the plaintiffs in error are in one sense a public corporation, the profits and benefits enure specially to the citizens of the South Ward, even to the extent it may be of
relieving them from municipal taxes. Surely it was never
intended that such a corporation should be exempt from all
taxation, while others are compelled to bear their share of
the public burden." While the law of this case is unsound
under practically all the authorities we have found, except
that of Kentucky, it is the legislature rather than the court
that is responsible for the inconsistent position taken by this
case. In providing that all property not expressly exempt
and especially that from which any revenue is derived
should be taxable, it is submitted that an erroneous distinction was made for the classification, for, under the argument
advanced earlier in this discussion and by the cases cited,
the fact that revenue is realized from municipal property
is not a sound basis for subjecting it to taxation.

[1] 94 Pa. St., 117.

CHAPTER VII

SALE OF MUNICIPAL PROPERTY PROVIDING PUBLIC UTILITIES

THE ease with which municipal corporations may conduct business enterprises is also dependent, but in an inverse ratio, upon the power which such corporations have to alienate their property. For experience has shown that in almost all cases private corporations stand ready to take over the operation of municipal public utilities where municipal corporations are becoming embarrassed or are reported to have made a failure of their operation. Indeed it has frequently been charged that influences have been brought to bear to secure an inefficient operation by municipal corporations of such public utilities with the purpose of cultivating among the people a feeling hostile to municipal and favorable to private operation.

The attitude of the courts in regard to recognizing the power in municipal corporations to dispose of municipal plants has therefore an important bearing on the answer to the question which is herein attempted, viz., What is the attitude of the courts toward an increase in the sphere of municipal activity?

The supplying of cities and towns and their citizens with such public utilities as gas, water or electric light for public and private consumption by the municipal corporation is the performance of a public duty, and the property so used is charged with a public trust and is devoted to a public purpose the same as other city property. Such property is dedicated irrevocably to the performance of this trust due the public and for its benefit and that of the inhabitants of the municipality. It is a fundamental principle that the trustee cannot disable itself from performing the trust by disposing of the property or means necessary to carry out the purposes of the trust relation without express authority from the party creating the trust or directing its administration. The power does not inhere in the trustee to defeat the carrying out of the trust by disposing of the trust property. The interests of the beneficiaries under the trust are guarded against any loss on this account by the courts holding that such property cannot be disposed of by the municipality unless under authority conferred specially by statute. The State alone, which attends to the matter of creating these trusts as well as to the selection of the trustees, has the power to provide for their destruction by sale or for their diversion as to trustees by lease or assignment. Having the sole power to create, the State alone has the ability to provide for a change of trustee or a winding-up of the trust entirely; so that in the absence of express legislative authority the courts refuse to imply the right in the municipal corporation, after having accepted the trust, to renounce its duties thereunder or to dispose of the trust property and thus defeat the further carrying out of the trust. The municipality must continue to perform the duties to the public after having once assumed the trust and undertaken to serve the public needs and those of the inhabitants.[1]

When the power to own and operate such plants for supplying public utilities has been given and accepted by a city, a franchise is conferred upon it for the purpose of securing some advantage to the public and for the benefit

---

[1] Dillon, *Municipal Corporations*, sec. 650.

of the inhabitants in their private capacity. Such beneficiaries have the right to complain in case of its reliquishment. This rule is based on the general principle of trusts as well as upon the rule that quasi-public corporations are formed in order to serve the public. The duty imposed is a personal one and the right to perform it together with the special privileges pertaining thereto is granted personally as a franchise, on condition that the grantee continue in personal control of such power and in the performance of its duties. The carrying out of the duties of serving the public under such a franchise is regarded as of special importance and the obligation is recognized as being peculiarily personal. Having selected a municipal corporation which is responsible and capable of executing the duties of the trust to the public for which are granted special privileges, amounting in most cases practically to a monopoly, the law does not permit the city to transfer its rights and the accompanying duties to another party which may or may not be responsible and capable of adequately serving the public and its inhabitants.

If at any time it may appear that the interests of the beneficiaries could be best served by some party other than the original grantee, the State which granted the franchise may in its discretion permit such change of grantees; but this must be provided for expressly by the statute. This rule of law is adhered to strictly because it is believed that the interests of the public are thereby subserved. For experience seems to have convinced the courts that the interests of the public are not the main object of private parties who engage in furnishing these public utilities. The desire for personal enrichment predominates over that of serving the best interests of the public. This fact necessitates that very extensive control be exercised over private grantees of such franchises or, what is still better security

that the public will be served adequately and at fair cost for
the service, makes it necessary that the public serve itself
directly or that it have the control which accompanies ownership, while the actual operation is provided for by a leasing of the plant owned by the city.   This matter, however,
is reserved for discussion after an examination of the authorities for the foregoing statements.

The case of Huron Waterworks Co. *vs.* Huron,[1] decided
in 1895, was an action to have an attempted sale of the
waterworks plant of the respondent city to the appellant,
a private corporation, declared void.   Such plant had before such attempted sale been owned and operated by the
city for supplying its public wants and for domestic purposes.   The question decided in the negative by this case
is as to whether the council of the city of Huron possesses
the power, unaided by the state legislature, to sell and transfer the Huron waterworks system to the appellant.   In
addition to the power given the city expressly by statute
to construct and maintain waterworks, the only statutory
authority granted provides, " that the city of Huron . . .
shall have power to make all contracts necessary to the
exercise of its corporate powers, to purchase, hold, lease,
transfer, and convey real and personal property for the
use of the city . . . and to exercise all the rights and
privileges pertaining to a municipal corporation."   In the
course of its convincing opinion the court, after citing and
discussing at length a number of leading authorities, expressed itself as follows: " Having, as we think, established the proposition that the waterworks of a city when
constructed and owned by the city, are to be regarded the
same as other city property held for public use, and therefore charged and clothed with a public trust, it would seem

[1] 7 S. Dak., 9.

to follow that such property cannot be sold and conveyed by the mayor and common council of the city unless under special authority conferred upon them to so sell and convey the same by the legislative power of the State. . . . From this examination of the authorities we conclude that there is no distinction between the nature of waterworks property owned and held by the city, and public parks, squares, wharves, quarries, hospitals, cemeteries, city halls, court-houses, fire engines, and apparatus, and other property owned and held by the city for public use. All such property is held by the municipality as a trustee in trust for the use and benefit of the citizens of the municipality, and it cannot be sold or disposed of by the common council of the city, except under the authority of the state legislature. . . . But such property is so owned and held by the municipality as the trustee of the citizens of the municipality, for the use and benefit of such citizens. It has been acquired by the corporation at the expense of the tax-payers of the city, for their use and benefit, and the law will not permit the corporation to divest itself of the trust, nor to deprive the citizens of their just rights as beneficiaries in the same."

The case of Lake County Water & Light Co. *vs.* Walsh,[1] decided in 1902, was an action to have set aside as fraudulent a deed of conveyance of the water and light plant of the city of East Chicago by said city to the appellant, a private corporation. In granting the relief asked for the court said in part: "It seems clear, upon the soundest reasoning and from the great weight of authority, that property held and used by a city for public purposes is held in trust for the inhabitants, and can not be sold or disposed of unless the city is specially authorized by the legislature

[1] 160 Ind., 32.

to make such sale or disposition and thereby determine
the trust. . . . The remaining question is whether waterworks and an electric light plant constructed or purchased
by the city and maintained by it for the extinguishment
of fires, for domestic purposes, for lighting the streets, and
for use in the houses of the inhabitants of the city are to
be regarded as property devoted to a public use. . . . The
right to furnish water for protection against fire, to clean
the streets, to flush sewers, and for the supply of the inhabitants, and the right to light the streets and public places,
and to furnish gas or electricity to the inhabitants, are
among the implied and inherent powers of a municipal corporation for the protection of the lives, health, and property of the inhabitants of the city, and, as to the lighting,
as a check on immorality. Unquestionably these are public purposes. . . . In our opinion waterworks and electric
light plants held, owned, and maintained by cities . . .
must be regarded as property held in trust for a public use.
Nor do we think they lose that character by reason of the
fact that water and light are supplied to the inhabitants for
domestic purposes, and that rentals and charges are paid
for the same."

In the case of New Albany Waterworks *vs.* Louisville
Banking Co.,[1] decided in 1903, the court refused the right
to the plaintiff, a private corporation, in the absence of express statutory authority, to lease to another like corporation the property, franchise and contracts of its waterworks
system, with which it was supplying water to a municipality
and its inhabitants. The case is mentioned in this
connection for the reason that the court indicated that it is
beyond the power of a municipality to validate such a lease
by its consenting thereto. The court said: " The final con-

---

[1] 122 Fed., 776.

tention in aid of the lease rests on the alleged assent thereto on the part of the city of New Albany. . . . The corporation is created by the state, and not by the municipality. While the latter may grant privileges to the corporation which are within their respective powers derived from the state, it can confer no authority upon the corporation to transcend those powers. The ordinance, therefore, is without force as authority for the lease."

The case of Ogden City *vs.* Bear Lake, etc., Waterworks Co.,[1] decided in 1898, was an action to set aside a lease of the waterworks plant while owned and operated by the plaintiff city, made by such city to the defendant, a private corporation. In finding such lease to have been made without authority and to be therefore void, the court used the following language: " Ogden City was a public corporation, and its authority was limited to such powers as were expressly granted by statute, and such as might be necessary to those expressly given. Undoubtedly, water distributed to a city and its inhabitants is devoted to a public use, and the entire system, whether consisting of reservoirs, conduits, pipes, or other means used to accomplish the delivery is also dedicated to the same use. The control and management of property dedicated to the use of the people of a city is given for their benefit, not for the individual benefit of the public authorities. . . . They cannot deprive the public of the benefit of property rights or powers affected with a public use by conveying or leasing it to others, unless their charter specially authorizes it, though such other corporation or person may undertake to give the public the use of it for compensation deemed reasonable. . . . When property whose use is devoted to the public is conveyed or leased to private corporations, though a contract may require its use to be given to the public for a rea-

[1] 52 Pac., 697.

sonable remuneration, the public, to a great extent, loses
its control over it, and any net income realized goes into the
hands and pockets of private parties. In fact, such parties
cannot give the use of their property to the public for the
actual cost of it, and the actual expense of the business, as
in this case. They must have profits, and it is to the
interest of such parties to make the profits or net income
as large as public officials will consent to make it. The
people usually get fleeced when the city places its waterworks in the hands of private parties. Public-spirited men
are not at all times free from the undue influence of self-
interest. Their disposition to favor the public is not equal
to their inclinations to favor themselves."

This case has been quoted from at length not only for
its clear enunciation of the principle of law at issue but especially for its discussion of the reasons for the decision
and for the practical attitude which the court takes in
dealing with the situation. That private gain is the controlling motive where such public-utility services are rendered by private capital is inevitable and this court seems
of the opinion that municipal ownership and operation are
necessary to secure proper service to the public and
the individual inhabitant. The case also takes the position,
although not necessary to the decision, that since the public
use of the property and the duty to the public are the
grounds for the principle of law laid down, where the
property of the city is not necessary or no longer suitable
for such use, it may be disposed of by the city. And it
is submitted this is a practicable limitation for the general
doctrine denying to the city the right by implication to
sell or lease its property acquired and used for public
purposes.

In the case of Ogden City *vs*. Waterworks & Irr. Co.,[1]

[1] 28 Utah, 25.

decided in 1904, the same court passed directly upon the
question of the exception to the general principle under
discussion in holding to be valid a lease made by the plaintiff city to the defendant of its waterworks plant which was
about to be abandoned by said city and was no longer capable of meeting the public and private demands made on
such a plant.   The decision gives the authority of law to the
dictum found in the earlier case referred to as decided by
this court, and is to be commended for its highly practical
treatment of the situation.   After finding the system to
have been insufficient the court adds that, "there is evidence in the record that tends to show that the system itself
had about outlived its usefulness. . . . In view of the conditions that existed and confronted Ogden City at the time
the lease was made, we are of the opinion that the city council not only acted within its authorized powers in authorizing its execution and afterwards ratifying it, but that, under the circumstances, those powers were wisely exercised,
for it is apparent that, after the city had decided to abandon its old waterworks system, it was necessary to make
some disposition of its water right; otherwise, in course
of time, it would be lost by nonuser."

This situation as to the actual condition of the property,
owned for the purpose of serving the public and having
become wholly unfit for the further giving of such service,
is even more strikingly found in the case of City of Indianapolis *vs.* Consumers' Gas Trust Co.,[1] decided in February,
1906.   The decision of this case held to be valid a certain
option given the appellant city by the respondent for the
sale of its gas plant with which it had supplied the inhabitants of the said city with natural gas.   This option to purchase had been given the city as a condition of its franchise

[1] 144 Fed., 640.

to the respondent company when the plant was originally installed and the city had given notice according to its terms of its election to exercise its rights to purchase the plant under such option.   At the time this action arose to enforce such sale the supply of natural gas had failed; so that this gas plant was not furnishing gas nor had it been in position to do so for several years.   To have held that such a sale was *ultra vires* because the company owed the duty of furnishing gas to the public would have been an unwarranted misapplication of a well recognized principle of law and a complete perversion of the purpose intended to be accomplished thereby, namely the protection of the public interests as against those of private parties.   In the nature of things it was impossible for the company to continue to supply the public so as to that purpose the plant was mere junk.   By purchasing the plant under its option the object of the city was to make possible the installation of an efficient artificial gas plant for the accommodation of the inhabitants of such city at a reasonable rate.   The court by Grosscup, J., said: " The thing enjoined by the court below [which is reversed here] was not the construction or operation of a municipal natural gas plant.   The thing enjoined was the purchase of dead mains and pipes—a purchase in the promotion of a purpose to construct and establish works that would distribute artificial gas—just such a public work as the statutes admittedly allow."

While this idle condition of the property was recognized by the court and must have had a material, practical effect upon its decision, the ground expressly given is the expiration of the franchise by the election of the city to purchase the plant according to its option, which the court found to be a valid condition to the granting of such franchise.   The court took occasion to draw the distinction between this agreement to sell a public-service plant to a municipality and agreements to sell to other parties, saying: " Examination of the numerous authorities cited for and against the contention of *ultra vires* reveals no case involving a provision of like character with this option clause, nor one in reference to a right to transfer the corporate property to a municipality under any circumstances. In none of the citations, state or general, are there any reasons stated that seem inconsistent with the proposition that a corporation, engaged in a service of public utility, may contract for a sale to the municipality of all of its property therein, either through a condition accepted in the franchise from the city, or through subsequent arrangement. The question whether municipal ownership is favorable to the public interest, is neither involved in, nor open to, judicial inquiry. Assuming that such ownership is authorized, and is contemplated or demanded by the municipality, we are convinced that this proviso, treated alone as a contract of sale on the part of the gas company, is not within the inhibition of the rule—not *ultra vires*. The public policy which is mentioned in the cases cited, as opposed to an implication of charter power to turn over its property to another and ' abnegate the performance of its duties to the public,' has no application to the transfer to the public— the municipality—of property used in public service." [1]

This distinction is supported by the common observation, made by this court, which is here recognized and given the effect of law, that the public interests in public-utility plants are so much more secure when controlled by public than by private capital that an agreement of a public or quasi-public corporation to sell to the one may be allowed, in the absence of express statutory authority, while the law

[1] The United States Supreme Court refused to reconsider this decision on a writ of certiorari, October 29, 1906, and thereby sustained such decision.

refuses to permit such an agreement to stand when made
with private parties. This must be the chief consideration for upholding the options to purchase such plants,
which are now so commonly taken by the municipality
when granting franchises. And such a precaution is a
very wise one for the city to take, for it provides the opportunity for the municipality at any time to take over
such property and control it absolutely for the public benefit. And while experience shows that this action is often
necessary the fact that it can be done so summarily acts
as an important factor in forcing public consideration into
the service rendered by the private concern.

These cases, then, will serve to show the general rule
of law, together with the practicable limitation placed
thereon by our courts, which denies to the municipality
the implied power to sell the property used in serving
the public, except when the public interest no longer necessitates its continued holding. And it should be noted, also,
that the rule is not limited to cases of voluntary sales but
that such property when used for public purposes is not subject to forced sales on execution.[1]

In the case of Bailey vs. Philadelphia,[2] decided in 1898,
the Supreme Court of Pennsylvania pretended to uphold
the power in the municipality to lease its gas works on the
theory that the city owned such property as a business corporation, and from this fact concluded that the city is not
required by its municipal duty under the statute to supply its
citizens with gas for lighting. The court, however, finds

[1] Dillon, *Mun. Corp.*, sec. 577; 5 Am. & Eng. Ency. Law, 1068, and
cases cited. The case of Sun Publ. Assn. *vs.* Mayor, 152 N. Y., 257, is
an interesting illustration of the principle that the municipality, when
expressly authorized, may lease such a public utility as a rapid-transit
system owned by the city.

[2] 184 Pa., 594.

that, "the right of alienation is given in express words in the charter." In so far as the actual decision of the case goes, in finding express statutory authority for the lease it is in full accord with the authorities, but the spirit of the case as shown by an extended argument which is *obiter dictum* tends to support the statement that the municipality has inherent power to lease or dispose entirely of its gas plant and that it is under no duty to serve the public with such a public utility beyond its own pleasure. This doctrine, which the case suggested, is not supported by the authorities but is directly contrary thereto, and its adoption would be dangerous to the public welfare; nor does it seem to have been followed by any of our courts.

CHAPTER VIII

POWER TO GRANT EXCLUSIVE FRANCHISES

THE attempt has been made to show in what has already been said that the courts favor both the recognition in municipal corporations of those powers whose exercise is necessary in order that such corporations may secure the ownership and operation of municipal public utilities and the adoption of the rules of law as to the taxation and sale of the property devoted to such purposes which will aid rather than impede such corporations in the adoption and pursuit of the policy of municipal ownership and operation.

The attempt has also been made to show that at least one of the motives which have led the courts to take the position they have assumed is their belief that private corporations are actuated by the motive of gain rather than public service. This same motive seems to have influenced the courts when they have been called upon to determine the legal relations which should exist between municipal corporations and private corporations where it has been decided to adopt the policy of private ownership and operation.

At the time when the exploitation of municipal public utilities was undertaken in this country it was believed that competition would secure to the public efficient service and reasonable rates from the private corporations which were entrusted with their operation. The courts therefore have striven to formulate the law in such a way that monopolies might not develop. They have hence held that munici-

pal corporations in the absence of statutory authorization
may not grant exclusive franchises for the ownership and
operation of public utilities. Furthermore the courts will
not so construe a franchise as to make it exclusive where
they can give it any other reasonable construction for fear
the public interest will be ignored for the sake of private
gain.[1]

But in the absence of the municipal ownership of plants
supplying these utilities it is necessary to depend on private
initiative for the service, and the erection and maintenance
of such systems require so large an outlay of money that
such enterprises will not be undertaken under contracts or
franchises running for short periods of time.[2]

It is necessary therefore to grant rather long contracts
before private capital will consent to launch such a business,
for it necessitates a large and a long-time investment because the property so acquired cannot be converted into
cash unless the statute expressly permits of its sale and
transfer to another, or unless the municipality itself be the
purchaser. To this extent the arrangement for providing
such service by private capital defeats the idea of keeping
the control constantly in the municipality. Notwithstanding, where it is found necessary to depend on private interests for these accommodations, the courts concede to municipal corporations the power by implication to make contracts for the supply of these utilities for public purposes
for a limited period, but in doing so the courts hold strictly
that such power does not include the giving of exclusive

[1] Little Falls Electric Co. *vs.* City of Little Falls, 102 Fed., 663; State
ex rel. vs. City of Hamilton, 47 Ohio St., 52; Hamilton Gaslight &
Coke Co. *vs.* Hamilton City, 146 U. S., 258; Thomas *vs.* City of Grand
Junction, 13 Col. App., 80; Illinois Trust & Savings Bank *vs.* Arkansas
City, 76 Fed., 271; Davenport *vs.* Kleinsmith, 6 Mont., 502.

[2] *Cf.* The City of Valparaiso *vs.* Gardner, 97 Ind., 1.

privileges for serving private purposes and individuals.[1]
By means of this reservation greater control is saved to
the municipality since it makes possible future competition
in the supply for private purposes. But this control is of
no great practicable value for the reason that these public
utilities are generally natural monopolies.

A discussion of some of the leading cases on this general question will serve to make these statements more au-
thoritative and will illustrate more fully the force and
practical effect of the principles herein enunciated.

The general principle is clearly expressed in the case of
Clarksburg Electric Light Co. *vs.* Clarksburg,[2] decided in
1900, in which the complainant claimed the exclusive right
to use the streets of the defendant city for operating an electric-light plant by virtue of a franchise granted by said
city and made in terms exclusive. In refusing relief to the
action which was to enjoin the erection of a competitive
electric-light system in said city the court spoke in the following manner: " Surely, we cannot say, contrary to the
drift of all the law of the country, that the mere power to
control streets and light the same carries with it by implication the enormous power to tie the hands of an important municipality for many years, or that such a power is
indispensable or necessary to enable the municipality to
carry out its legitimate functions. Therefore, the council
of Clarksburg had no authority to grant this exclusive
franchise; and that feature of its ordinance is *ultra vires,*
and therefore, void, confers no right [and] makes no
contract."

[1] Gas Co. *vs.* Parkersburg, 30 W. Va., 435; Long *vs.* City of Duluth,
51 N. W., 913; National Foundry & Pipe Works *vs.* Oconto Water Co.,
52 Fed., 29; Detroit Citizens' Street Ry. Co. *vs.* Detroit, 110 Mich., 384.

[2] 50 L. R. A., 142.

In the case of Smith *vs.* Town of Westerly,[1] decided in 1896, the court, in construing a statute empowering any city or town to grant to any person or corporation the right to erect waterworks therein to supply its inhabitants with water, said: " It will be seen at once that, in attempting to grant to said company the exclusive right to lay water pipes in the public highways of the said town, the town council exceeded the authority conferred by said statute, and hence that the town is not bound by said contract; for, however it may be as respects the power of the legislature to make such a grant exclusive, it is clear that no such power can be exercised by a town council unless it is conferred by express words or by necessary implication."

The law on this question is shown to be fundamental and of long standing in the opinion of the court of North Carolina in the case of Thrift *vs.* Elizabeth City.[2]   In construing a municipal ordinance the court said: " Those provisions of the ordinance granting the exclusive privilege to construct and maintain waterworks within the corporate limits of the town, and the exclusive use of its streets, alleys, sidewalks, public grounds, streams, and bridges, come within the condemnation of sec. 1 of the Constitution of this state, which declares that ' perpetuities and monopolies are contrary to the genius of a free state, and ought not to be allowed.' . . . All authorities hold that no such exclusive privilege can be granted by a municipal corporation without express legislative authority."

The case of Citizens' Gas etc. Co. *vs.* Town of Elwood,[3] also contains a well reasoned decision on this principle of law where it is said: " The town trustees had no authority to grant the Elwood Natural Gas and Oil Company the exclusive right to use the streets of the town. A municipal

[1] 35 Atl. (R. I.), 526.   [2] 122 N. C., 31.   [3] 114 Ind., 332.

corporation cannot grant to any fuel or gas supply company
a monopoly of its streets.   There is nothing in the nature
or business of such a company making its use of the streets
necessarily exclusive.   The spirit and policy of the law for-
bid municipal corporations from creating monopolies, by
favoring one corporation to the exclusion of others.   It is
probably true that a municipal corporation may make a contract with a gas company for supplying light to the public
lamps for a limited time, even though it be for a number of
years; on this point, however, there is some conflict, but
there is no conflict on the proposition that, in the absence
of express legislative authority, a municipal corporation
can not grant to any corporation the exclusive privilege of
using its streets."

And finally the Supreme Court of the United States in
the case of Freeport Water Co. *vs.* City of Freeport,[1] has
said: " The power of a municipal corporation to grant exclusive privileges must be conferred by explicit terms.   If
inferred from other powers, it is not enough that the
power is convenient; it must be indispensable to them."

While the municipal authorities are given power by implication to contract for the supply of public utilities to the
city beyond their term of office and for a reasonable time
because it is practically impossible to get such a contract
to any advantage and for a reasonable compensation for
short periods, what is a reasonable time for such contracts
is a question of fact to be determined in each case.   No definite period of time can be fixed upon as a reasonable one
for all cases.   The decision of the question depends upon
so many varying circumstances and conditions as to situation, cost of supply and future prospects that our courts
will not interfere to set aside such contracts made by cities

[1] 180 U. S., 587.

in the exercise of their discretion except in extreme cases of its abuse.

The case of Westminster Water Co. *vs.* Westminster,[1] decided in 1904, holds void a perpetual contract for the water supply of the defendant city. The opinion contains a brief summary of some of the cases deciding what are reasonable periods for such contracts. It thus shows that, " in the case of New Orleans Waterworks Co. *vs.* Rivers,[2] a contract for fifty years was sustained; in Walla Walla *vs.* Walla Walla Water Co.,[3] a contract for twenty-five years was sustained; in Vicksburg Waterworks Co. *vs.* Vicksburg,[4] a contract for thirty years was held not unreasonable."

The case of City of Vincennes *vs.* Citizens' Gas Light Co.,[5] expresses this well established principle by saying: "A city has power to contract for a supply of gas or water for a stated period of time extending beyond the tenure of office of the individual members of the common council making such contract. . . . We cannot say that twenty-five years is an unreasonable time for which to contract for a supply of light or water."

Finally it is the rule of the courts that a franchise will not be so construed as to make it exclusive if any other construction is possible even where the municipal corporation granting it has by statute the right to grant an exclusive franchise. The case of City of Meridian *vs.* Farmers' Loan & Trust Co.,[6] decided in 1906, was that of an injunction sought for the purpose of restraining the appellant city from exercising the powers conferred upon it by a statute, passed after its contract with the assignor of the respondent for supplying said city and its inhabitants with

[1] 64 L. R. A. (Md.), 630.
[2] 115 U. S., 674.
[3] 172 U. S., 1.
[4] 185 U. S., 65.
[5] 132 Ind., 114.
[6] 143 Fed., 67.

water, to erect and operate a new plant for the purpose of
supplying itself and its citizens with water. In refusing to
grant the relief prayed for and to concede to the respondent
the exclusive right to supply water for the public and private demands of the city by virtue of said contract, the court
said: "The contract does not contain any provision by
which the city expressly agreed not to establish and operate
a waterworks plant of its own during the period of the
existence of the contract between it and the Meridian
Waterworks Company. The relief prayed for could only
be granted upon the theory that the law under the circumstances will supply by its implications the want of an express agreement that the city would not build waterworks
of its own. We need not consider what would be implied
in the case of a contract like this between private parties.
The contract here is one in which a municipal corporation
makes a grant in which the public has an interest. When
a municipal corporation is exercising its functions for the
public good, it is not to be shorn of its right to continue to
exert its powers for the general good by mere implication.
If by contract it may under the circumstances restrict the
exercise of its public powers, the intention to do so must
be shown by apt words so clear as not to reasonably permit
any other construction. Unless there can be found in the
contract in question words clearly depriving the city of
Meridian of the right to build, own, and operate waterworks, the court should not by implication give such effect
to the contract." [1]

A recent decision of the Supreme Court of the United
States directly on this question is found in the case of
Knoxville Water Co. *vs.* Knoxville,[2] decided in 1906, where

[1] See also Water, Light & Gas Co. *vs.* City of Hutchinson, 144 Fed.,
256; City of Joplin *vs.* Southwest Missouri Light Co., 191 U. S., 150;
Re Brooklyn, 143 N. Y., 596.   [2] 200 U. S., 22.

the action was to enjoin the defendant city from erecting and operating a waterworks system in competition with that of the plaintiff, who claimed the exclusive right to render such service by virtue of a contract wherein the said city agreed, ' not to grant to any other person or corporation, any contract or privilege to furnish water to the City of Knoxville or the inhabitants thereof for a period of thirty years.' In speaking of this contract the court said: " We fail to find in it any words necessarily importing an obligation on the part of the city not to establish and maintain waterworks of its own during the term of the water company. . . . The stipulation in the agreement that the city would not, at any time during the thirty years commencing August 1st, 1883, grant to any person or corporation the same privileges it had given to the water company, was by no means an agreement that it would never, during that period, construct and maintain waterworks of its own."

But even where the statute does not permit the municipal corporation to grant an exclusive franchise, the courts still hold that it may preclude itself by the terms of a franchise from itself entering into competition with its grantee. The case of Walla Walla *vs.* Walla Walla Water Co.,[1] decided in 1898, is the leading one illustrating this principle of law. In sustaining an agreement on the part of the city, made under proper statutory authority for securing the supply of these public utilities by private capital, which expressly excluded the municipal corporation for the period of the franchise from engaging in competition with such private enterprise in supplying these utilities to itself and its inhabitants, the court took the position that it was in effect nothing more than an express promise to carry out the agreement of its franchise to the company in good faith;

[1] 172 U. S. 1.

and held that such a limitation on its own power did not
amount to the granting of a franchise exclusive of all competition which the charter of the city in question expressly
provided could not be done.

The case of Vicksburg *vs.* Vicksburg Waterworks Co.,[1]
decided in May, 1906, is concerned with the question under discussion in the two former cases and its decision is
based expressly on the Walla Walla case. The court indicated its intention to give full credit to the authority of
the Knoxville Water Co. case by saying: "And unless the
city has excluded itself in plain and explicit terms from
competition with the [private] waterworks company during
the period of this contract, it cannot be held to have done
so by mere implication. The rule, as applied to waterworks
contracts, was last announced in this court in Knoxville
Water Co. *vs.* Knoxville."[2] The court by Day, J., then pro-
ceeds to find in the franchise under construction in the
case, an agreement binding on the city which excluded it
from owning and erecting such a plant during the period
of such franchise by virtue of the fact that it had been made
in terms exclusive for such period. The court said: "We
cannot conceive how the right can be exclusive, and the
city have the right, at the same time, to erect and maintain
a system of waterworks which may, and probably would,
practically destroy the value of rights and privileges conferred in the grant."

From this holding Harlan, J., who wrote the opinion in
the Knoxville Water Co. case, dissented, giving as his
reason for so doing that, " it ought not, in my judgment,
to be held upon the present record that the city has by ordinance or otherwise, precluded itself from establishing
and maintaining, at its own expense, a system of water-

[1] 202 U. S., 453.   [2] 200 U. S., 22.

works for the benefit of its people. The contrary cannot be maintained, unless we hold that a municipal corporation may, by mere implication, bargain away its duty to protect the public health and the public safety as they are involved in supplying the people with sufficient water. Nothing can be more important or vital to any people than that they should be supplied with pure wholesome water. And yet, it is now held that it was competent for the city of Vicksburg, by mere implication, to so tie its hands that it cannot perform the duty which it owes in that regard to its people."

In the interest of municipal activity and for the better safeguarding of the welfare of the people living in cities, it is to be regretted that this highly practical position of Justice Harlan was not sustained by the prevailing decision in this case which, it would seem, in effect seriously attacks, if in fact it does not virtually overrule, the principle established in the Knoxville Water Co. case.

CHAPTER IX

MUNICIPAL REGULATION OF RATES FOR PUBLIC UTILITIES

THE courts, while holding that competition has great value in securing the public advantage in case of the operation of public utilities by private capital, have at the same time felt that it was unwise to trust to it alone. They have therefore endeavored to secure to municipal corporations the right to regulate private capital engaged in rendering public service where the exercise of such a right was consistent with a due regard to the private rights guaranteed by the constitution and with the general principles of the laws regulating the powers of municipal corporations.

The rule of law is now universally accepted that when private property is devoted to a public use, it is subject to public regulation and control. Property is clothed with a public interest and devoted to a public use when used in a manner to make it of public consequence, and to affect the entire community. When one devotes property to a use in which the public has an interest, he virtually grants to the public an interest in that use, and must submit to public control for the common good to the extent of the interest so granted.[1]

It is evident that when the State in the exercise of its sovereign power grants a charter, conferring the privilege of existing and operating as a legal entity upon the united interests of a number of individuals and constituting them

[1] Munn *vs.* People of Illinois, 94 U. S., 113.

a body corporate, such a grant of special rights and privileges can be made subject to such conditions and regulations as the State may see fit to impose within constitutional limitations. Being the creature of statutory origin, the corporation possesses only the powers given by such origin upon the conditions stipulated by the State. And where the power to alter, amend or repeal is reserved in connection with the granting of the charter, such power may be exercised at any time thereafter without impairing the obligation of contracts, prohibited by our Federal Constitution, because the contract resulting from the acceptance of the franchise is made subject to such modification or rescission.[1] As stated by the Supreme Court of Indiana in the case of Hockett *vs.* The State,[2] " the power of a State Legislature to prescribe the maximum charges which a telephone company may make for services rendered, facilities afforded, or articles of property furnished for use in its business, is plenary and complete."

But this power of the State to regulate, which includes the power to fix the maximum rates that may be charged for the service, is a sovereign power which our courts hold can be delegated to municipal corporations only in express terms or by necessary implication. While the legislature has the right to fix the price at which gas, water, or electric lights shall be supplied by one who enjoys a monopoly of the business by reason of having such exclusive privilege, the courts will not presume such right to be vested in the municipality unless it has been granted by the Legislature expressly or by clear implication.

The case of In re Pryor,[3] decided in 1895, establishes this principle. After granting a franchise to erect and

---

[1] Spring Valley Water Works *vs.* Schlotter, 110 U. S., 347.
[2] 105 Ind., 250.   [3] 55 Kan., 724.

maintain a gas system within its limits, without prescrib-
ing any rates to be charged for the supply of such gas for
domestic purposes, upon which grant such a system was installed, the city of Iola, Kansas, nine years after granting
the franchise, passed an ordinance fixing the maximum
rates to be charged for such service at much less than those
theretofore charged. In denying the validity of such ordinance attempting to fix the rates for such service the
court said: " The act providing for the organization and
government of cities of the third class [to which Iola be-
longed] contains no express grant of power to fix or regulate the prices of gas, water or any other article of necessity
or luxury. . . . Certainly there is no express authority
conferred upon the municipal authorities by this section to
regulate the price of gas or water [providing general powers in corporations to provide cities with gas or water ' with
the consent of the municipal authorities thereof, and under
such regulations as they may prescribe.'] Whether they
might as a condition of their consent, provide that gas or
water should be furnished to the city or to its inhabitants
at not exceeding certain prescribed rates, we do not now
inquire. Consent was granted by ordinance No. 268,
to the Iola Gas and Coal Company, its successors
and assigns [of whom petitioner is assignee] without an-
nexing any condition as to rates. . . . In certain cases the
State may fix and regulate the prices of commodities and
the compensation for services, but this is a sovereign power,
which may not be delegated to cities or subordinate sub-
divisions of the State, except in express terms or by necessary implication. No such power is expressly conferred
upon the cities of the third class, and we do not think the
right can be implied from any express provision, unless
possibly that in the grant of consent to any person or corporation so to use the streets and public grounds of the

city a condition might be imposed as to the maximum rates to be charged."

To this same effect is the case of Webaska Electric Co. *vs.* City of Wymore,[1] decided in 1900, on an action to restrain the enforcement of an ordinance reducing rates for electric light furnished by the plaintiff under a franchise from the defendant city. The Court said: "In dealing with this feature of the case it is not necessary to determine whether the city was authorized by its charter, as it existed in 1889, to grant any person, company or corporation, an exclusive franchise for the erection and operation of an electric light plant. The plant has come into being; it is now established, and the owner thereof has the right to furnish light to its private customers on such terms as may be mutually satisfactory to the parties concerned. The defendant has plainly no power or authority to regulate the plaintiff's charges for lights furnished to the inhabitants of Wymore. The Legislature has, of course, the right to fix the price at which gas or electric lights shall be supplied by one who enjoys a monopoly of the business by reason of having an exclusive franchise; and such right may be delegated to the governing body of a public or municipal corporation. But the power of regulating the charges for electric lights is not found among the grant of powers contained in defendant's charter. There is no such authority given, either expressly or by implication and, therefore, it does not exist."

The same principle is equally applicable to, and has been fully enunciated in connection with, the giving of telephone service in municipalities which has practically all of the elements of a natural monopoly. As early as 1888 in the case of City of St. Louis *vs.* Bell Telephone Co.,[2] the court

[1] 60 Neb., 199.   [2] 96 Mo., 623.

laid down this rule of law as follows: " This was a prose-
cution against the Bell Telephone Company of Missouri
for the violation of an ordinance which provides that the
annual charge for the use of the telephone in the city of
St. Louis shall not exceed fifty dollars. . . . The important question, then, is whether the city of St. Louis has the
power to enact the ordinance in question. . . . If the city
has such power it must be found in a reasonable and fair
construction of its charter. . . . That the company is subject to reasonable regulations prescribed by the city, as to
planting its poles and stringing its wires and the like, is
obvious.   Such regulations have been obeyed by this defendant.   Conceding all this, we are at a loss to see
what this power to regulate the use of the streets has
to do with the power to fix telephone charges.   The
power to regulate the charges for telephone service
is neither included in nor incidental to the power to
regulate the use of streets, and the ordinance cannot
be upheld, on any such ground. . . . The power to
regulate, it may be conceded, gives the city the right to
make police regulations as to the mode in which the desig-
nated employment shall be exercised.   But taking these
charter provisions together, we think it would be going
to an extreme length to say that they confer upon the city
the power to fix telephone rates. . . . We conclude that
the city has no power to pass the ordinance in question by
reason of any of the charter powers before considered. . . .
To say that under this general power [of the general welfare clause] the city may fix rates for telephone services
would be going entirely too far." [1]

   This same principle with reference to the power of cities

---

[1] This principle was fully affirmed by the same court in 1905 in State
ex rel. vs. Telephone Co., 189 Mo., 83.

to regulate the rates for telephone service only in those cases where the right to do so has been expressly conferred upon the municipality or can be necessarily implied from some express grant by the State, is clearly stated together with the reason on which the rule of law is based in the case of State ex rel. The Wisconsin Telephone Co. *vs.* City of Sheboygan,[1] decided in 1901. In the course of its opinion the court said: " Whatever power a municipality possesses over the wires and poles of a telephone company in its streets must be granted it by the legislature—2 Dillon, Mun. Corp. Sec. 698. The charter of the city of Sheboygan empowers it to enact proper ordinances and regulations for the government and good order of the city for the benefit of trade and commerce for the suppression of vice and the prevention of crime, to prevent the incumbering of streets, to provide for the removal of obstructions therein, to regulate the manner of using streets, and to protect them from injury. As we have already seen, this grant of power does not authorize the city to wholly prevent the relator from doing business within its limits. No express authority is given the city to regulate charges for telephone service, nor is there any express grant of power, from which such authority can necessarily be implied. . . . The power to regulate charges was not included in or incidental to the power to regulate the manner of using streets. There is not the remotest relation between them. The attempt of the city to justify its position on that ground must fail. . . . Neither does the power come to the city under the general authority to pass ordinances for the government and good order of the city and for the benefit of trade and commerce. To say that under this general power the city may fix rates for telephone service would be going entirely too far."

[1] 111 Wis., 23.

The Supreme Court of Indiana in a series of recent decisions has firmly established in that state this principle
as to the municipal regulation of rates for public utilities
in connection with the matter of supplying natural gas to
the inhabitants of municipalities. The first case of Lewisville Natural Gas Co. *vs.* State ex rel.,[1] was an action to
compel the appellant company by mandamus to furnish gas
at the price fixed by an ordinance of the town of Lewisville
by the terms of which the said company was required to
furnish gas at a lower price than it had been charging
for such service. In deciding the question as to the power
of said town so to fix the price at which the appellant should
supply the citizens with gas, the court said: " It is not
contended that the general statute upon the subject of in-
corporating towns confers upon towns, when incorporated,
the power to regulate the price at which natural gas shall
be sold. It is contended, however, that such power is
conferred by an act of the General Assembly, approved
March 7, 1887. That act is as follows: ' Section 1. Be
it enacted, etc., That the boards of trustees of towns, and
the common councils of cities, in this State, shall have
power to provide by ordinance, reasonable regulations for
the safe supply, distribution and consumption of natural gas
within the respective limits of such towns and cities, and
to require persons or companies to whom the privileges of
using the streets and alleys of such towns and cities is
granted for the supply and distribution of such gas to pay
a reasonable license, for such franchise and privilege.' . . .
There is not a word or a syllable to be found in this act
indicating that the General Assembly had in view any other
purpose than that of securing the safe supply and use of
natural gas. To secure the safe supply and use of natural
gas is one thing and to fix the price at which gas shall

[1] 135 Ind., 49.

be supplied is another and quite different thing. In our opinion it was not the intention of the General Assembly to confer, by the act above set out, the power to regulate the price at which natural gas should be furnished. . . . The trustees of the town of Lewisville having no power to regulate the price at which natural gas should be furnished, the ordinance in question, purporting to do so is void upon its face."

The decision of this case is expressly affirmed by the same court in 1901, in the City of Noblesville *vs.* Noblesville Gas etc., Co.,[1] where the court said: " It would be doing violence to the rules of statutory construction to hold that under the law of 1887 [quoted *supra*] the power of a city, when not reserved in granting a franchise, to prescribe the prices chargeable by its licensee to consumers of its gas, is free from fair and reasonable doubt."

In this case the appellee company had instituted an action to enjoin the appellant city from enforcing an ordinance regulating the rates to be charged consumers of natural gas. It appeared that the franchise originally granted said company gave no exclusive right and fixed no time for its continuance and imposed no restrictions upon the price to be charged for gas either by express stipulation or a reservation to fix or control prices thereafter. The ordinance passed by the city later fixed the maximum rates in particular cases that might be charged by any one accepting its provisions, which the appellee company did expressly in writing duly filed with the common council of said city. In deciding the case on this point in favor of the city the court said: " That the city had no power to regulate the rates of its licensee makes no difference. It had the power to contract. And the power to regulate as a

1 157 Ind., 162.

governmental function, and the power to contract for the
same end, are quite different things. One requires the
consent only of one body, the other the consent of two.
In this instance the city acted in the exercise of its power
to contract, and it is therefore entitled to the benefits of
its bargain. There is no merit in appellee's contention that
the ordinance of 1888 fails for want of consideration. Appellee's original franchise of 1886 was without restriction
as to rates; and it could have continued to enjoy its franchise and fix its own rates (if reasonable) if it had chosen
to do so. By the ordinance of 1888 the city in effect proposed that any person, firm or corporation, including appellee, desiring the use of its streets and alleys as a means
of marketing natural gas, might have the same, by under-
taking to abide by and perform all the conditions set forth,
including the limitation upon prices for gas. Appellee was
not required to accept the new proposition. It might have
gone on without a contract for chargeable rates, and taken
its chances of legal interference, or it might free itself
of uncertainty by accepting the certainty of contract. It
chose the latter course, accepted the ordinance, and for
the first time had a contract and a legal authorization to
charge the price specified in the ordinance contract. This
was a sufficient consideration."

This contractual power of municipalities to impose regulations in the matter of rates to be charged for gas when
the company agrees to accept the same, and by so doing en-
ters into a contract of its own motion, is further defined
and established in the case of Muncie Natural Gas Co. *vs.*
City of Muncie.[1] This was an action to restrain the violation of a contract under which the appellant company
was given authority by the respondent city to maintain and
operate a natural gas system in said city and to supply gas

[1] 160 Ind., 97.

at not to exceed the maximum rates stipulated in said contract. To the defense of said company that such contract was *ultra vires* the city and therefore void because no power was vested in it to enter into such a contract fixing the rates to be charged its inhabitants for gas, the court held that, since the company had continued to use the streets of said city for the distribution of natural gas to private consumers by virtue of such contract, it was not within the power of the company to deny the right of the city to enter into such a contract.

But in the course of its opinion the court expressed the belief that there was no lack of power in the city to make such a contract, saying: " Natural gas is a public utility that cannot be obtained by the citizens of a municipality generally, except as it is conducted in pipes along the public ways of the city. The grant of exclusive power to the common council over such ways comprehends the right to permit gas companies to use the streets. If the common council may permit a natural gas company to use the streets without any condition annexed, except such as the law attaches, it is not perceived why, as in this case, in making provision for supplying natural gas to all of the inhabitants of the city, it may not protect such inhabitants against extortion by providing that the company shall not charge in excess of certain prices for its service. . . . It was not limited alone to the granting of this franchise, but it had the right to prescribe and impose terms and conditions. When these terms and conditions . . . were accepted . . . it became a binding contract."

To what extent the city has power to insist on stipulations, regulating rates or fixing the maximum price which might be charged by a company for its gas, in negotiating a contract for the granting of a franchise to such a company when it refuses to accept such stipulations and be bound in the matter of rates, this case does not decide. And while the expressions of the opinion above set out would indicate that the attitude of the court favors the holding that such power belongs to the municipality even when no express authority has been delegated to it to fix rates, this position was not necessary to the decision of the case and so cannot be regarded as having the authority of law. While there is good reason for holding the city to have the power to prohibit the charging of excessive rates in connection with the granting of its franchise just as the courts will enjoin the company from making extortionate charges for its service, it is submitted the city cannot fix the rates to be charged under the mere general authority to regulate the use of its streets. To permit them to do so would have the effect of denying the validity of the well established principle that such power belongs to the city only when the grant of it is found to have been made by the legislature expressly or by necessary implication. The court limits the application of its remarks, however, by saying that " municipalities cannot, under existing legislation, exercise the legislative power to fix rates in any case."

This principle is further discussed and its application more clearly defined in the case of City of Rushville *vs.* Rushville Natural Gas Co.,[1] which was decided in 1905. The appellee in this case was in occupation of the streets and public places of the city of Rushville and was supplying its inhabitants with natural gas, under a franchise granted for that purpose by an ordinance of said city passed in July, 1889, known as No. 26, which imposed no restrictions or limitations upon said appellee with respect to the rate to be charged consumers for such gas, or as to the method by which the price should be ascertained and fixed. In August 1890, the appellant city duly passed another ordin-

[1] 164 Ind., 162.

ance, known as No. 30, granting generally to any corporation, firm, company or individual a franchise to supply said city and its inhabitants with natural gas upon compliance with certain terms and conditions. And in May, 1899, said city passed a third ordinance known as No. 73, amending said ordinance No. 30 by providing for the use of meters for the measurement of the gas consumed and limiting the charge therefor to fifteen cents per thousand feet. The action in the case was brought by the appellant to enjoin the appellee from increasing its rates and charging consumers of natural gas in excess of the maximum price fixed by the provisions of said ordinances Nos. 30 and 73. The court stated the principle in question in the following decisive language:

"Appellee accepted the provisions of this ordinance [No. 26], adjudged and conceded to be valid, and constructed its plant at a cost of $100,000 to fulfil the purpose of its creation. The acceptance by appellee of the privileges granted by appellant in this ordinance constituted a contract equally binding upon both parties, and when acted upon rights became vested, and its provisions became secure against impairment by any subsequent municipal action. . . . This ordinance did not prescribe any limits as to charges for gas, or reserve to the city the right thereafter so to do. No alteration of or addition to the terms of the contract thus formed could be made afterwards by either party without the consent of the other. . . . It is now the settled law of this State that, under such circumstances as shown here, cities have no authority or power by subsequent ordinance or action, to impose any additional restrictions regulating the price to be charged for gas furnished under such contract."

In the case of Mills *vs.* City of Chicago,[1] decided in 1904,

[1] 127 Fed., 731.

the action was to restrain the enforcement of an ordinance of the defendant city forbidding manufacturers from demanding more than seventy-five cents per thousand cubic feet for gas served to its customers, which was a marked reduction from the prevailing price of gas. In refusing to find such power in the city to regulate the rate of gas supply the court said: " No one has pretended that the regulation of the price of gas is essential to the specific object for which the city of Chicago was created. . . . It is plain to me that the sixty-sixth section, while granting power to regulate the police of the city or village, cannot be enlarged to include power to regulate the price of gas. . . . The mere laying of gas pipe, and the installation of gas plants, together with their repair, are the subject matter of a power widely separable in circumstance from the power to deal with the rates at which gas shall be manufactured and sold. The first belongs naturally to the city whose streets are to be occupied, for it is related intimately with the supervision of streets; the latter, with equal reason, is foreign naturally to the city. . . . Until there is legislation, more unmistakable than the language used in this section, to indicate a purpose to grant the city power to fix rates, I shall not hold that such was the legislative intent. Unquestionably the power resides somewhere in the State, but until consciously delegated to some other body, it remains in the State's general repository of power, the General Assembly of the State."

And finally the case of State ex rel. City of St. Louis *vs.* Laclede Gas Light Co.[1] was a mandamus action to compel the respondent company to comply with an ordinance of the relator city and supply gas to consumers at not to exceed ninety-five cents per thousand cubic feet, being a reduction from one dollar and twenty-five cents per

[1] 102 Mo., 472.

thousand. In denying such power in the city by virtue of the police power vested therein, the court expressed its opinion in the following clear language: " It is not open to doubt or dispute that this power to make and vend gas carries with it as an inevitable incident the right to fix the price of the gas thus made and sold. . . . So that, by the terms of the charter of the respondent company its right to fix the price of its product was as much a part of its charter as if it had been in terms set forth in section 5 of the original act of incorporation. But, if a price had thus been set forth, no one familiar with constitutional principles but would at once deny that the right to contract for the sale of gas at such price could anywise be impaired. . . . But certainly there is a limit in this regard over which legislatures and municipalities cannot pass; they cannot, in the exercise of assumed police powers, violate charter contracts and overthrow vested rights. On this subject Judge Cooley aptly says: ' The limit to the exercise of the police power in these cases must be this: The regulations must have reference to the comfort, safety or welfare of society; they must not be in conflict with any of the provisions of the charter; and they must not, under pretense of regulation, take from the corporation any of the essential rights and privileges which the charter confers. In short, they must be police regulations in fact, and not amendment of the charter in curtailment of the corporate franchise.' "[1]

Where authority is expressly conferred upon the municipality to fix the rates at which public utilities may be supplied to its inhabitants by private capital, the courts agree that such municipality may fix these rates but they must be

[1] Cooley, *Constitutional Limitations*, 5th ed., 712. See also Tacoma Gas and Electric Co. *vs.* Tacoma, 14 Wash., 288; Omaha Water Co. *vs.* City of Omaha, 147 Fed., 1.

reasonable; for the state cannot by itself or any of its
agencies deny to the owners of private property a fair return for its use at a just valuation. To permit this would
amount to a deprivation of property without due process of law. The principle is stated to be the general rule of
law by the Supreme Court of the United States in the
leading case of San Diego Land, etc. Co. *vs*. National
City,[1] and in many other cases. In the course of this opinion the court defines what constitutes " reasonable rates "
as follows: " What the company is entitled to demand, in
order that it may have just compensation, is a fair return
upon the reasonable value of the property at the time it is
being used for the public."

Where the rates fixed by the municipality acting under
proper authority are not reasonable, redress may be had by
the party injured at the hands of the courts for they stand
ready on good cause shown to enjoin the enforcement of
an ordinance reducing such rates below what is fair and
reasonable. The fixing of rates, however, is a legislative
act requiring the exercise of discretion and will not be interfered with by the courts unless, as is said in the case
just referred to, " they are so plainly and palpably unreasonable as to make their enforcement equivalent to the taking
of property for public use without such compensation as
under all the circumstances is just both to the owner and
to the public." As this same court has said in another
case: " The extent of judicial interference is protection
against unreasonable rates." [2]

[1] 174 U. S., 739.

[2] 143 U. S., 339. To the same effect and for the further definition of
the term, " reasonable rates," see San Diego Water Co. *vs*. San Diego,
118 Cal., 556; Brymer *vs*. Butler Water Co., 179 Pa., 231; Des Moines
vs. Des Moines Waterworks Co., 95 Ia., 348; Capital City Gaslight Co.
vs. Des Moines, 72 Fed., 829; New Memphis Gas & Light Co. *vs*. Memphis, 72 Fed., 952; State *ex rel. vs*. Cincinnati, etc., Co., 18 Ohio St., 262.

The case of Milhau *vs.* Sharp [1] decided as early as 1854 that a statute, providing that certain municipal corporations should have the power from time to time to regulate the rates of fare to be charged by street railway companies could not be defeated in its operation by a resolution of any such municipality forever waiving such power by a perpetual grant to a certain company to erect and operate a street-railway system in Broadway, New York City. In perpetually enjoining such action by the company for the reason that such resolution was void the court said: "An ordinance regulating a street is a legislative act, entirely beyond the control of the judicial power of the State. But the resolution in question is not such an act. Though it relates to a street, and very materially affects the mode in which that street is to be used, yet, in its essential features, it is a contract. Privileges exclusive in their nature, and designed to be perpetual in their duration, are conferred. Instead of regulating the use of the street, the use itself, to the extent specified in the resolution, is granted to the associates of the Broadway railroad. . . . The licenses contemplated by the resolution must therefore be regarded as perpetual and irrevocable. If it takes effect at all, the right of way, now vested in the corporation, so far as it is necessary for the purposes of the defendants, will become vested in them. The exercise of the legislative powers of the corporation, in respect to that street, must be in subordination to the vested rights of the defendants. We have already seen that a corporation cannot, without the consent of the legislature, thus divest itself of its own powers. The resolution itself is, therefore, unauthorized and void."

[1] 17 Barb. (N. Y.), 435.

CHAPTER X

Conclusions

In what has been said the endeavor has been made to indicate what has been the attitude of our courts toward the question of the municipal ownership and operation of public utilities by showing what have been their decisions on the points of law which affect both the power of municipal corporations to extend their sphere of activity and the facility with which they might exercise the powers pertaining to this general subject which are regarded as inhering in them.

By way of stating the conclusions which have been reached it may be said 1st. Municipal ownership and operation is regarded by the courts as quite consistent with our constitutional system. There is no constitutional objection to the grant by the legislature of the widest powers relative to the municipal ownership and operation of public utilities. Only one case casts any doubt upon the power of the legislature to permit a municipality to enter into the field of business. This is Opinion of the Justices [1] which regards as improper the attempt of the legislature to permit a city to establish yards for the sale of coal and wood. The courts further have given the widest possible meaning to the term "municipal purpose" in our constitutions where by the terms of those instruments cities were forbidden to exercise the power of taxation or to spend public funds for other than such purposes.

[1] 155 Mass., 598.

2nd. The courts have further with few exceptions in their consideration of the powers possessed by municipal corporations adopted the principle of liberal construction where its adoption was necessary to permit the corporations to extend their sphere of activity in order to render to their inhabitants the services so necessary in modern urban life, and have with this purpose in view developed the idea of powers implied from the very nature of such corporations as organs for social service.

3d. With the idea that municipal corporations, which have entered into what is often called the field of private business, are really discharging a service which is just as public in character as the preservation of the peace, the care of the public health and safety or the care of the poor, the courts have also refused to make any distinction between the property used for these so-called commercial purposes and that used for the so-called governmental purposes, and have therefore denied that one class of property is to be taxed any more than the other or is to be governed by any more liberal law as to its sale or alienation. The courts do not of course take the view that it is not subject to taxation or alienation but merely that as property devoted to a public service it is untaxable and inalienable in the absence of statutory provisions to that effect.

4th. With the same idea in view, that what we call public utilities are public whether in public or in private hands, the courts have assumed that the interests of the public must be the guiding influence upon them in their decision as to the powers possessed by municipal corporations in the grant to private companies of these public utility franchises.

Believing whether mistakenly or not that much advantage will accrue to the public from competition in the operation of public utilities, the courts have not favored exclusive franchises and have refused both to recognize the power of municipal corporations in the absence of statutory authority to grant exclusive franchises and to imply any exclusiveness in a franchise where any other reasonable construction was possible in case it was recognized that the corporation granting the franchise had the legal right to make it exclusive.

5th. Believing finally that competition alone would be ineffective to secure reasonable rates in an industry which in the nature of things is largely monopolistic in character, the courts have regarded the legislature as possessed of the power of regulating the rates that might be charged by public-service corporations. They have at the same time, either because they feared too drastic action by municipal corporations or because of a reluctance to abandon the rule of strict construction of municipal charters, denied that a municipal corporation had the right, in the absence of statutory provision to that effect, to regulate these rates except where it had reserved to itself such power to regulate in the franchise at the time of its grant.

In laying down these rules the courts have been strongly influenced by the feeling that the controlling motive of the private companies was that of the pecuniary advantage of their stockholders, and that unless checked this motive might result to the public disadvantage. On the other hand they have frequently called attention to the fact that the motive actuating municipal corporations was public service rather than private advantage. They have therefore recognized that in the absence of legislative authorization a private company operating a public utility might sell out to a municipal corporation, although a municipal corporation could not reverse the process.

While finally the courts have naturally not been called upon to decide the expediency or inexpediency of the policy of municipal ownership and operation of public utilities, since they have regarded the decision of this question in concrete cases as not a judicial matter but rather a question for the municipality concerned to decide for itself within the limits of the statutes, they have in a number of instances not hesitated to voice the feeling that the trend of modern thought was favorable to municipal ownership and operation.

In the case of Mayo *vs.* Town of Washington,[1] decided in 1898, Clark, J., in a dissenting opinion which is later expressly upheld by the court in the case of Fawcett *vs.* Mt. Airy,[2] in speaking of the relation of the court to the matter of municipal ownership and of the tendency of such ownership to become more fully established in practice, says: " It would seem, however, that city ownership of water as well as electric lighting plants is a matter vested in the discretion of the city government. Light and water, sewerage and sanitation, paving and fire protection are necessities, and are objects to be obtained by municipal organization. . . . There is an unmistakable trend the world over toward municipal ownership of lighting, waterworks, and even (to some extent) street railways. Judge Dillon refers to this, and intimates that it is commended by wisdom and sound policy.[3] In Germany two-thirds of the cities own their electric lighting and car plants, and the proportion is increasing. The same is true of the other countries of continental Europe, there being a great increase in municipal ownership since Judge Dillon wrote. In Great Britain and Ireland 203 cities and towns, being in fact every city of any importance save 5, own their lighting plants, not only for their own corporate uses, but for furnishing light to citizens, and the average price of gas

[1] 122 N. C., 5.   [2] 134 N. C., 125.
[3] Dill., *Mun. Corp.*, sec. 691, note 1.

furnished to the citizen, with a profit, too, to the municipalities is 54 cents per thousand. In this country, too, a large number of cities own their gas plants. . . . A large and increasing number of cities and towns (already over 200) in the United States, own their electric lighting plants, with the result that the cost to the municipalities, from official reports, is less than one-third of the average cost in cities buying their lights from private companies. The number of cities in this country owning their waterworks is 1690 out of a total of 3196 having water supply; and municipal ownership is steadily increasing. In the 50 largest cities in the Union, 19 have recently changed from private ownership to municipal ownership, leaving only 9 of the 50 which are still dependent for their water supply on private companies. . . . The general movement of the age in which we live is towards the ownership and operation of these franchises by the people of towns and cities, for themselves, through the agency of their municipal corporations, as one of the recognized and chief purposes of town and city charters."

This case has been quoted from at length for its statistical value especially and for the conclusions drawn by the Justice after an apparently extensive study of the question. The facts speak for themselves and indicate that the municipal ownership of the plants providing these public utilities in towns and cities was widely established at the time of the writing of this opinion, and that the tendency as indicated by such facts is toward a rapid increase of such ownership.

In the decisions of the courts in connection with this subject no suggestion is found indicative of anything but the utmost confidence in the principles involved, nor are any reasons assigned for denying their broadest application in practice. And the attitude of the courts on such a subject, it is believed, gives the most conservative and accurate indication of the tendency of the times and of the probable solution of the question.

That the public interests are best conserved by municipal ownership is fully recognized and forcibly expressed by the court in the case of Ogden City *vs.* Bear Lake, etc., Waterworks Co.,[1] to the effect that, " the people usually get fleeced when the city places its waterworks in the hands of private parties. Public-spirited men are not at all times free from the undue influence of self-interest." But whether the municipality finds that the amount of control necessary in any case requires the municipal ownership of the plants which provide it and its citizens with these public utilities, or only the ownership without the operation by the public, or merely the statutory regulation of private plants, it is submitted on the authorities herein given that the attitude of our courts favors a decided increase in the sphere of municipal activity.

[1] 52 Pac., 697.

LIST OF AUTHORITIES.

Alpena City Water Co. *vs.* Alpena, 90 N. W., 323.
Altgelt *vs.* City of San Antonio, 81 Tex., 436.
American and English Encyclopædia of Law.
Atlantic City Waterworks Co. *vs.* Atlantic City, 6 Atl., 24.
Austin *vs.* Coggeshall, 12 R. I., 329.
Avery *vs.* Job, 25 Ore., 512.
Bailey *vs.* Philadelphia, 184 Pa., 594.
Baumgartner *vs.* Hasty, 100 Ind., 575.
Belding Improvement Co. *vs.* Belding, 128 Mich., 79.
Blanchard *vs.* Village of Benton, 109 Ill. App., 569.
Blood *vs.* Electric Co., 68 N. H., 340.
Brick Presbyterian Church *vs.* City of New York, 5 Cowen, 538.
Brymer *vs.* Butler Water Co., 179 Pa., 231.
Capitol City Gas Light Co. *vs.* Des Moines, 72 Fed., 829.
Cartersville Waterworks Co. *vs.* Cartersville, 89 Ga., 689.
Chadwick *vs.* Maginnes, 94 Pa. St., 117.
Champer *vs.* City of Greencastle, 138 Ind., 339.
Christensen *vs.* City of Fremont, 45 Neb., 160.
Citizens Gas, etc., Co. *vs.* Town of Elwood, 114 Ind., 332.
City of Covington *vs.* District of Highlands, 113 Ky., 612.
City of Crawfordsville *vs.* Braden, 130 Ind., 149.
City of Ft. Scott *vs.* Eads Brokerage Co., 117 Fed., 51.
City of Henderson *vs.* Young, 83 S. W., 583.
City of Indianapolis *vs.* Consumers' Gas Trust Co., 144 Fed., 640.
City of Joplin *vs.* Southwest Missouri Light Co., 191 U. S., 150.
City of Louisville *vs.* Commonwealth, 62 Ky., 295.
City of Meridian *vs.* Farmers' Loan and Trust Co., 143 Fed., 67.
City of Newport *vs.* Newport Light Co., 84 Ky., 166.
City of Noblesville *vs.* Noblesville Gas, etc., Co., 157 Ind., 162.
City of Owensboro *vs.* Knox's Admr., 116 Ky., 451.
City of Rushville *vs.* Rushville Natural Gas Co., 164 Ind., 162.
City of St. Louis *vs.* Bell Telephone Co., 96 Mo., 623.
City of St. Paul *vs.* Laidler, 2 Minn., 190.
City of Shelbyville *vs.* The Cleveland, etc., Ry. Co., 146 Ind., 66.
City of Somerville *vs.* City of Waltham, 170 Mass., 160.

Janeway *vs.* City of Duluth, 68 N. W., 24.
Knoxville Water Co. *vs.* Knoxville, 200 U. S., 22.
Kyle *vs.* Malin, 8 Ind., 34.
Lake County Water & Light Co. *vs.* Walsh, 160 Ind., 32.
Lawrence *vs.* Methuen, 166 Mass., 206.
Lehigh Water Company's Appeal, 102 Pa., 515.
Levis *vs.* City of Newton, 75 Fed., 884.
Lewisville Natural Gas Co. *vs.* State *ex rel.*, 135 Ind., 49.
Linn *vs.* Borough of Chambersburg, 160 Pa., 511.
Little Falls Electric Co. *vs.* City of Little Falls, 102 Fed., 663.
Logan Natural Gas & Fuel Co. *vs.* City of Chillicothe, 65 Ohio St., 186.
Long *vs.* City of Duluth, 51 N. W., 913.
McBean *vs.* City of Fresno, 112 Cal., 159.
Mauldin *vs.* Greenville, 33 S. C., 1.
Mayo *vs.* Town of Washington, 122 N. C., 5.
Mayor, etc., of Rome *vs.* Cabot, 28 Ga., 50.
Mealey *vs.* Hagerstown, 92 Md., 741.
Merrimack River Savings Bank *vs.* Lowell, 152 Mass., 556.
Metcalf *vs.* City of Seattle, 25 Pac., 1010.
Middleton *vs.* St. Augustine, 42 Fla., 287.
Milhau *vs.* Sharp, 17 Barb., 435.
Miller *vs.* Fitchburg, 180 Mass., 32.
Mills *vs.* City of Chicago, 127 Fed., 731.
Mitchell *vs.* City of Negaunee, 113 Mich., 359.
Montgomery Gas Light Co. *vs.* City of Montgomery, 4 L. R. A., 616.
Muncie Natural Gas Co. *vs.* City of Muncie, 160 Ind., 97.
Munn *vs.* People of Illinois, 94 U. S., 113.
National Foundry & Pipe Works *vs.* Oconto Water Co., 52 Fed., 29.
National Tube Works *vs.* City of Chamberlain, 5 Dak., 54.
Negley *vs.* Henderson, 22 Ky. L. R., 912.
New Albany Waterworks *vs.* Louisville Banking Co., 122 Fed., 776.
New Decatur *vs.* Berry, 90 Ala., 432.
New Memphis Gas & L. Co. *vs.* Memphis, 72 Fed., 952.
New Orleans Waterworks Co. *vs.* Rivers, 115 U. S., 674.
Newport *vs.* Commonwealth, 106 Ky., 434.
Newport *vs.* Unity, 68 N. H., 587.
Norwich Gas & Electric Co. *vs.* Norwich, 76 Conn., 565.
Ogden City *vs.* Bear Lake, etc., Waterworks Co., 52 Pac., 697.
Ogden City *vs.* Waterworks & Irr. Co., 28 Utah, 25.
Opinion of the Justices, 150 Mass., 592.
Opinion of the Justices, 155 Mass., 598.
Parsons *vs.* Van Wyck, 56 App. Div. (N. Y.), 329.
Penley *vs.* City of Auburn, 85 Me., 278.
People *ex rel. vs.* Assessors of the City of Brooklyn, 111 N. Y., 505.

VITA

Oscar Lewis Pond, author of this Dissertation, was born
in Shelby county, Indiana, March 25, 1877, and received
his preliminary education in the common schools of that
county and in the Shelbyville high school. He entered
Indiana University in 1895, and graduated in 1899 in the
Department of History and Political Science with the degree of Bachelor of Arts. He entered Columbia University
in 1899, and received the degree of Bachelor of Laws in
the year 1902. He also received the degree of Master of
Arts from Columbia University in 1902, having studied in
the School of Political Science. His major subject was
Constitutional Law, under Professor Burgess; his minor
subjects were Criminal Law under Professor Houston, and
Science of Finance under Professor Seligman. He continued his studies in the School of Political Science in 1902,
hearing lectures also under Professors Goodnow, Munroe
Smith, and Giddings. He was made a member of the
Indianapolis Bar in 1902, and became Professor of Law in
the Indianapolis College of Law in 1903.